Contents

MAKING MORE MONEY

Using
Value
Analysis

DONALD E. PARKER

ISBN: 1492338737

ISBN 13: 9781492338734

Library of Congress Control Number: 2013916395
CreateSpace Independent Publishing Platform
North Charleston, South Carolina

Acknowledgments

I am an engineer who has been practicing in the field of value analysis for 40 plus years. Although I am not directly experienced in manufacturing I am surrounded by experts in manufacturing through SAVE International. I owe many thanks to the following industry professionals from whom I have assembled the expertise expressed in their books and papers to join with my knowledge of value analysis to create this work.

The following individuals have worked, or are working, for a manufacturing company and are certified value specialists (CVS®) or associate value specialists (AVS) of SAVE International:

Lawrence D. Miles – General Electric
Sanjay S. Gaikwad - Whirlpool
Arthur E. Mudge – Joy Manufacturing
Theodore C. Fowler – TRW
James R Vickers - Raytheon
Carlos Fallon – RCA Corporation
Jim Rains – General Motors
Joseph Otero – Pratt & Whitney
Don J. Gerhardt - Ingersoll-Rand
James D. Bolton – Whirlpool
Yuh-Huei Jo Chang – China Engineering Consulting
Ching-Song Liou – China Engineering Consulting

The following individuals are industry consultants:

Warren J. Ridge
J. Jerry Kaufman
Gary R. Myers
James R. Wixson
John E. Sloggy
Jay Mandelbaum

The following individuals are manufacturing representatives:

Bob Roller – Cree
Samuel Maya - GlaxoSmithkline

Thank you to my editorial team for their valuable assistance – my wife, Mary Frances and my daughters – Ann Mutersbaugh and Katherine Rollins.

Preface

My recently published book titled: *Working on What Matters, a value analysis solution,* has a picture of two arrows on the cover – a green one pointed upward called **revenue** and a red one crossing it pointed downward called **expense.**

The sequel, this book delves a bit deeper into the details of how to improve the cash flow from your business by exploring the meaning and pitfalls of revenue, expense, and their contribution to value.

Does revenue from a business mean gross income, net income, fixed income, variable income, interest, dividends, loans, and distributions of stock or profit? The answer is yes. It means all types of money.

Does expense of a business mean gross expense, net expense, fixed expense, variable expense, capital expense, overhead, general and administrative (G&A), committed funds, contracted obligations, and declining stock prices? Again, the answer is yes to all of these.

The formulas are simple:

Revenue > Expense = Profit
Revenue < Expense = Loss

You can use value analysis (VA) (sometimes called VE – value engineering) to achieve three options – increase revenue to be greater than expense, decrease expense below the revenue you are getting, or break even to survive another day.

In order to do this one must understand the nuances of each of the types of revenue and expense and how they interact with each other. If you can recognize all expenses and sunk costs and evaluate their worth then you have achieved the first step toward reducing them and improving value. Also if you can recognize revenue sources and how they can be changed or increased you will benefit. This book will not make you an accountant but it will increase your awareness of the things you can do to improve your business using VA tools to help you make more money.

To avoid being repetitive when I refer to an "article," "widget" or "it" in this book I am referring to a manufactured product or a provided service – both of which will result in revenue when sold to the client and have expenses to achieve the sale.

Read each Chapter carefully to learn *its secret message to making more money!*

Donald E. Parker, PE, CCE, CVS®

CHAPTER I

What is Price?

The greatest influence on price is what the market will bear.

Everyone who wants to survive in business must know the definition of price and how it is determined. Here is the old definition that many currently still use:

Price = Cost + Profit

This is an accounting expression. "Price" is the "seller's/producers" expectation of what the "buyer/consumer" will pay for the benefits gained by the acquisition. Those benefits are called "Worth." Therefore, you have a sale when it is perceived that the acquisition "is worth the price."

1

The new expression for price in the Global economy is:

Price - Profit = Target Cost[1]

The older model worked well before global competition. The timing for global competition is different based on the industry. For automobiles it was the 1980's. For appliances like Whirlpool it was the late 1990's, with the entry of Korea and then China into the North American marketplace. For others it is just starting to happen, or has happened within the past few years.

The new formula is based on the premise that price is determined by the marketplace or customer, not the manufacturer. Due to the current intense global competitive marketplace, manufacturers are no longer able to determine the sales price. Essentially, most manufacturing companies now know this. They have also learned that LEAN and Six Sigma do not move the needle enough to get them to become competitive, so they have learned that VA/VE is the best method to use to attack cost.

✲✲✲

Regardless of the definition used, it is interesting what the dictionary[2] says about price. Synonyms for price are given as – charge, cost, expenditure, expense and outlay. What that means is that the price you set and receive should at least be at minimum what it cost you to obtain or create the product, so you won't lose money!

The cost of a thing is all that has been expended upon it; whether in discovery, production, refinement, decoration, transportation, or otherwise, to bring it to its present condition in the hands of its present possessor. The price of a thing is what the seller asks for it, and it becomes what you pay for it.

What you cannot forget if you want to make money is that the seller's price is now your cost – what you pay to obtain it (raw

---

1 *Target Cost Management, The Ladder to Global Survival and Success,* Jim Rains, CRC Press, 2011, pg xvii.

2 *Random House Webster's unabridged dictionary,* 2nd edition, 2001.

materials for example or a subcontracted part). When a person pays for something, that person is determining its value. So if you set your price too high, for whatever reason, and you've sunk cost into it and forgone any profit, you have lost money if it doesn't sell.

✳✳✳

Value[3] is the monetary or material worth of an item, whether the item is for sale or not. The market value is what something would bring if it were for sale in the open market. Its intrinsic value is the inherent worth of the article considered alone. For example, the market value of an old and rare volume may be very great, while its intrinsic value may be nothing.

Charge, mentioned above as a synonym for price has special reference[4] to services, expense to outlays; as in the charges of a lawyer or physician, traveling expenses, etc.

✳✳✳

Where this leads is the fact that all products and services provide a function that is purchased by a buyer for a price he or she is willing to pay.

A function is the reason something is wanted.[5] It is the purpose for the product. In VA, functions are expressed by using a **verb** and a **noun.** For example, the reason someone might buy a car is to **transport people.** Well, if the price of a car is $30,000 – is it worth $30,000 to **transport people**? If you buy it, it is. If, however, you choose to rent a car for $300 a month to **transport people** – achieving the function is then not worth $30,000 to buy the car.

What the methodology of value analysis (VA) does is to define the function obtained by the acquisition of the product or service

---

3 ibid
4 ibid
5 Pocket Guide, *Value Methodology*, Goal QPC, 2008

and to set the price to be paid against the function (rather than the product or service) to see if the expense is worth it.

Where the expense of attaining a function is not worth the price, a value mismatch has been identified.

A business executive who knows the prices set by competitors and benchmarks the price of those functions, is determining the worth of his/her prices. Of course, this is what the buyers of products and services also need to do more of – evaluate the worth of the functions they are obtaining.

Some people may want something at any price. The vast majority of us do not! Most of us want to separate needs from desires to make our money stretch further. Allocating the money we have to spend to the functions we want to achieve is the essence of value analysis.

The secret message in this -

You can lower your price, make the same profit, become more competitive and make more money using value analysis.

CHAPTER 2

What is Profit?

We hope you get all you need without sacrificing sales!!

Profit is a necessary if you want to expand your business, conduct research, invent new products, and earn money for yourself and your investors. Even though consumers are always looking for bargains they accept paying a "reasonable" mark-up for goods and services they buy.

Profit is not necessary if you want to just break-even, keep all your employees employed, pay yourself a living wage, keep up with the cost of inflation of your material and supplies, and maintain the status quo in sales volume. This occurs when you bid or accept a contract to provide products or services at a price just enough to cover your costs. That's the staying in business, feed your family syndrome. Value analysis is not in that business.

It recognizes the vital need to make profit to grow, as long as the amount of profit is not greedy.

The dictionary[6] has the following synonyms for profit: return, net income, good, advancement, and improvement. Our focus in this text is for profit to be in the form of cash rather than gaining good, helpful or useful benefits.

In this context, the returns or receipts include all that is received from any outlay or investment. The profit is the excess (if any) of the receipts over the outlay. Profit is the return from employment of capital after deducting the amount paid for raw material and for wages, real or estimated rent, interest, insurance, etc.

Profit is that sum of the amount received for goods and services which exceeds the sum originally paid for them, with or without secondary expenses involved. It is also the income of invested property without counting its increased value by any actual rise in the market. In invested capital, profit is the ratio of the increment to the actual amount of capital for a given year. Here is the definition of two commonly used terms:

- **Gross Profit**
  The profit apparent on the face of a transaction or business
  The excess of sales over receipts for expenditures or purchases
- **Net Profit**
  The surplus remaining from gross profit after all necessary deductions, as for interest, transportation, bad debts, credit card fees, and other expenses

---

6 ibid

Jim Rains points out in his book[7] that profit is different from profit margin. He has seen where higher profit margin actually generates a lower profit. This occurs when annual volume of sales is low, but each sale has a higher profit margin.

If the price were lower and more competitive in the marketplace, the increased sales would greatly generate more profit for the company. He cites a case where a 20% profit margin was reduced to 10% resulting in 20 times more sales volume with 8 times more profit.

The real major question left is what is a "reasonable" profit? The answer to that is in the eye of the beholder and customer, and it often varies by market segment. For construction changes, it seems a 5-8% profit is acceptable to tack on a change order. For investors, they seem to want profit in the double digit range because of risk they feel they are taking in letting you use or in loaning you the money. For retailers, they seem to be in the 40-50% profit range, so they can offer special sales and discounts while dealing with rejects and returns.

Regardless of the formal definitions of profit, to me – profit is all the money you have left over after having paid all bills and obligations for the products and services you are selling.

So, for a value analyst,[8] profit is that increment of cost you can add to all your other costs to achieve a price for the **functions** you are selling that the market will bear.

Conventional wisdom indicates that there are four ways to make more money from the business you have:

- Sell more (assuming you are making a profit)
- Reduce expenses on what you are selling
- Raise prices (assuming that will not harm sales)
- Lower prices (assuming you have increased sales to make more profit)

---

7 *Target Cost Management, The Ladder to Global Survival and Success,* Jim Rains, CRC Press, 2011, pg 68.

8 A certified value specialist (CVS®) by SAVE International

Practicing value analysis can increase your performance on these four things plus add a couple of other opportunities to make money:

- Develop better value new products
- Obtain market advantage through reduced user costs (life-cycle)

✱✱✱

Larry Miles, known as the father of value analysis, says in his book,[9] "In a free enterprise system, with competition at full play, success in business over the long term hinges on continually offering the customer the best value for the price asked. Competition, in other words, determines in what direction one must go in setting the value content in order for a product or service to be competitive."

"This best value is determined by two considerations: *performance and cost.*" The product or service must do what it is needed to do, for as long as it is needed to do it. Also, its cost must be acceptable to the consumer over its life cycle of use.

One major company has defined its product attributes[10] that are major performance characteristics that matter to its customers. These attributes are:

- Aesthetics – Appearance of the product from the customers viewpoint
- Capacity – Usable space of the product on primary functional dimensions

---

9 *Techniques of Value Analysis and Engineering, 3rd edition,* Lawrence D. Miles, Eleanor Miles Walker, Executive Director, The Value Foundation, 1989, pg 5.

10 2013 SAVE International Conference paper titled, *Product Leadership by integrating Product Attributes with Function Analysis,* Sanjay S Gaikwad, CVS®, NAR/US Regional Manager, Design For Value, Whirlpool Corporation

- Core Performance – Degree to which a product fulfills purchase drives for customer benefits, functions and related claims
- Craftsmanship – Fit and feel of the product
- Energy – Energy usage (efficiency, consumption, or comparison) and related claims
- Installation & Logistics – Requirements from end of line, through distribution channels and into customer homes
- Noise & Vibration – Requirements relating to product sound output (level and quality), vibration input into dwelling, audible feedback, and closure signatures
- Reliability – Basic quality requirements of operating life (usually 1, 4, and 10 yrs)
- Service – Requirements regarding ease of service and diagnostics
- Usability – Requirements related to operating product for intended functions
- Safety & Codes – Compliance to agency, regulatory, and internal requirements

Sanjay Gaikwad's paper crystallizes the integration of product attributes with function cost to determine the value objectives that the company desires to offer to its customers. The paper describes how 55 alternatives were developed resulting in 8 alternative product concepts for a Top Washer glass lid subsystem. This resulted in savings significant enough to pass the "Winning Definition Tollgate," which is an essential first step in the product development process at Whirlpool to launch a new product.

By understanding customer needs better than your competition and delivering solutions to meet those needs better than anyone else, you can achieve product leadership. Product leadership is when more customers make the decision to buy your product over competitive products. Product leadership is driving businesses to profitable growth through product innovation.

Value analysis can make you more money when you consider required performance and cost together.

The secret message in this -

You can increase your profit, reduce your price and reduce your cost by using value analysis.

CHAPTER 3

A look at expenses

Expenses can be planned, obligated or
real for decision making.

One of the best value analysts in industry that I knew was Art Mudge who worked as Vice President – Value Planning for Joy Manufacturing Company. He knew that you needed an understanding of your project's direct and related costs. I will lean on his book[11] for the types and categories of cost involved in bringing a product to market.

He stated that first you must know the **prime costs** related to the product. Prime costs are the direct material and labor costs charged to a specific manufactured product, job order or part order as they are incurred.

---

11 *Value Engineering, a systematic approach,* Arthur E. Mudge, 1981, 2nd printing, pgs 53-54.

These costs must be in two forms: first, they should show a total for the complete project under analysis and second, they should be segregated as labor and material for each of the assemblies, subassemblies and parts of the project.

They should include and break out the costs of any indirect material or labor expended on the project; tooling costs, including the cost of special jigs and fixtures; boxing, packaging, and shipping cots; and any other special costs involved.

✳✳✳

A typical generalized cost structure is shown below. Read this table from left to right to see the cost elements included in each category.

Selling price	Profit				Cost of goods sold
	Selling costs				
	General administrative costs				
	Field service and miscellaneous costs	Overhead costs	Conversion costs	Cost of goods manufacturing	
	Indirect labor				
	Indirect material				
	Direct labor	Prime costs			
	Direct material				

Generalized Cost Structure

The **overhead costs** shown in the chart are also known as indirect costs or burden. They are apportioned to a manufactured product, job order, or part order from an indirect cost account into which they have normally been segregated.

These overhead accounts cover costs such as development, supervision, tooling, maintenance, heat, power, light, buildings, taxes, etc. They are distributed to specific orders in proportion to a base such as direct labor cost (most common), direct labor hours, equipment hours, or any number of others depending on the nature of the operation.

General and administrative (G&A) and overhead are very similar. There can be separate costs for home overhead and field overhead. These are normally calculated annually and are expressed as a percentage of the previous years' business volume.

For most manufacturers G&A costs are often called "indirect" costs because they are not directly billable to the cost of a specific job or contract. Some manufacturers, however, are now trying to collect and allocate indirect costs to a specific product. Billable hours, normally in the service industry, are those time-carded and/or charged to the specific work being done for a client for a specific product, project or service.

✳✳✳

One day at work I heard that higher level management announced a new policy that henceforth all employees would be required to have at least 70% billable hours (this was a design firm with an audited 150% overhead rate). I didn't understand this directive because I was working full-time for a set of clients doing value studies, conducting training, writing study reports, etc. My billable hours were 100% that year. So, I went to my boss and said, "Looks like I can screw around 30% of the time (1-1/2 days out of a 5 day week)! Needless to say that didn't work.

Non-billable hours are those hours allowed to employees for vacation, jury duty, sick leave, training, etc. that cannot be charged to any specific job, client work or contract. Management executives, secretaries, accountants and similar staff who work on all jobs fall into the non-billable time of an organization. The cost for this non-billable time is calculated each year, added to the business overhead rate, and recouped the next year by adding that overhead rate across the organization to all the work being done.

For example, every person has the potential for 2,080 hours of work each year (40 hrs per week times 52 weeks). If you are given 10 Federal holidays and 2 weeks vacation your available time to work is now 1,920 hours or a decrease of 7.7%. If you are earning $52,000 per year your employer must charge your time to a client at a rate of $56,004 a year to make up for your time off which is not billable. Of course, if you don't time card and charge the project you are working on the full 1,920 hours in a year because you took sick leave, went to a conference, attended staff meetings, etc., your overhead rate just increased.

✹✹✹

Conversion costs, as explained by Art Mudge, are the monies expended in effort and indirect material required to convert the raw material (direct material) into the desired usable item.

✹✹✹

Another type of cost classification of interest in VA work is that of costs shown as **fixed** or **variable** cost. These are often referred to as non-recurring and recurring costs. Variable or recurring costs are those which the company continues to pay for as long as they are in production. Fixed costs are often viewed as non-recurring, one-time costs.

Fixed costs are normally expressed as a lump sum dollar amounts. This type of cost is often accrued before a product is made or a service is given. When this occurs, it is referred to as "sunk" cost (see Chapter 5). It is money invested whether or not you make a product or give a service.

Also, fixed cost can exist in the form of longer term obligations during manufacturing of a product or the execution of a service. If you are obligated by lease, contract or loan agreement to pay a sum of money over a period of time, this is a fixed cost whether or not you make a product or provide a service. The obligation also makes it sunk cost that is not recoverable unless you are released of the obligation.

The common types of fixed costs are shown in the two lists below. These costs are not all inclusive or exclusive to each list but may be combined as appropriate for the endeavor being considered.

A look at expenses

Common Fixed Costs for Products	Common Fixed Costs for Services
Facilities	Rent
Design	Development
Tooling	Equipment
Prototype	Initial Training
Testing	Research
Publications	Contracting
Set-up	G&A
Overhead	

✷✷✷

Variable costs are often expressed as unit costs that recur as production continues and services are given. Variable costs can go to zero if production and services stop. Any residual materials and equipment left over after production and services stop is now considered a fixed sunk cost.

The common types of variable costs are shown in the two lists below. These costs are not exclusive to each list but again may be combined as appropriate.

Common variable costs for Products	Common variable costs for Services
Labor	Advertising
Materials	Staffing
Packing	Supplies
Inspection	Delivery
Shipping	Monitoring
Storage	Repair
Fuel, Power	Utilities
Maintenance	

This list of variable cost elements assumes one can separate the cost element for the product or service from the same cost element for the general business endeavor. For example, do you meter the utility cost to run a production line for widgets separately from the utility cost to run the whole building? Another example, do you have separate cost for the storage of raw materials or inventory of the one product you are making or is that cost combined with many other products?

A cost is only variable if it comes and goes with the volume of production or service.

***

The majority of VA in industry is product oriented. It is applied to the material and labor content of a product that will be delivered to a user or customer. Ted Fowler in his text,[12] states that "the most dramatic value analysis studies attack those items that one commonly refers to as burden, overhead, or SG&A (selling, general and administrative)."

He indicates three primary reasons for the power of such an analysis:

- These costs are allocations, that is, are grouped together and allocated to an account. This process serves to disguise their identity.
- They are seldom effectively analyzed except to compare differences in cost ratios.
- The overhead value analysis team usually comprises the top operating manager and his or her staff. The function viewpoint permits these decision makers a new and uncommonly focused viewpoint.

"The users and customers of overhead are primarily those within the organization who regularly interact with and benefit from the activities funded by the overhead accounts." Don't let this divert you from seeking out how to reduce overhead.

---

12 *Value Analysis in Design, competitive manufacturing*, Theodore C. Fowler, Van Nostrand Reinhold, N.Y., 1990, pg 26.

Overhead is a secondary function to the primary function of the product. The customer is buying primary function. The customer for your product really does not want to pay for your overhead.

✳✳✳

One of the biggest expenses that is largely in the overhead cost category is paperwork that must be created, read by someone, filed and stored. Warren Ridge[13] aptly described this phenomenon "The Paperwork Menace."

He goes on to say that in 1968 there were 35,000 computers in the country each capable of spewing out a stack of records 20 feet high each day. In 1971, Robert Kunzig, Administrator of the U.S. General Services Administration, speaking before his Regional Commissioners, said that "computers should bring an end to the need for file cabinets," and that he expected GSA to "significantly reduce the number of file cabinets in the agency" if he let them have computers.

That never happened! Now we have millions of computers in the country as well as more advanced speed printing and thousands of file cabinets to spend money on – putting in and taking out paper. Today, no one is keeping track of the effort spent storing information on hard drives, CD's, thumb drives, and a myriad of other devices. Warren Ridges' paperwork menace has become the information menace, and its unchecked usage continues to drive up overhead costs. That is no way to make more money!

✳✳✳

Most companies know how to make a work break-down structure (WBS) of their products and assign costs to the whole product, and then to each major product system, and then to each subsystem of the major systems – all the way down to the cost of components for each subsystem. Yet rarely do they make a WBS

---

13 *Value Analysis for Better Management,* Warren J. Ridge, American Management Association, Inc., 1969, pgs 17-29.

of the overhead costs they use to increase the direct and variable costs of their products.

I have seen overhead costs as low as 50% and as high as 150% applied to the cost to produce a product. The recapture of funds expended on overhead is a necessity, but it also directly increases the price a customer has to pay and reduces the value of the product.

When I worked as an employee a few years back I made an annual salary of $80,000 a year. At a 150% overhead rate the company had to charge the client $200,000 a year for my time. I often wondered if I was worth that amount of money, and why I wasn't paid that and wondered if the rate that was being charged for my time limited the amount of work the client paid us to do. It didn't make me feel that I was worth $200,000 a year!

***

The typical eight departments in a manufacturing company can be depicted as:

Company Departments			
Engineering	Purchasing	Manufacturing	Marketing
Research	Warehouse	Shipping	Sales

If you have additional or different departments then modify the above list. The key is to break-down your overhead rate for the company by major departments. The sum of all the overhead cost of the individual departments should equal the sum of the overhead costs for the company. If field overhead is also involved, include that as a separate cost category in the above chart. Create a WBS of overhead for each department with at least the three categories of cost shown below - personnel, facility, and other costs:

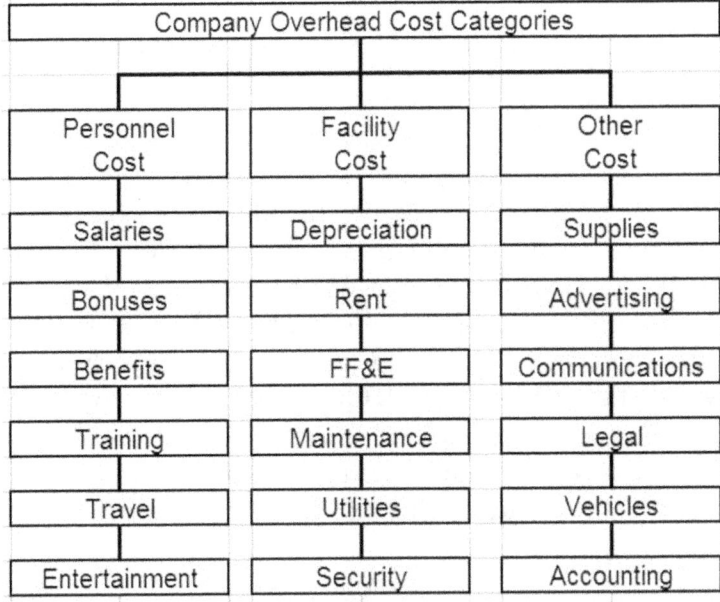

Of course you should break-down personnel costs by executive and management functions and supporting functions like receptionist, clerical, administrative, data entry, filing, etc.

Also, there are any number of methods to allocate the annual cost contribution to overhead of the facilities and furniture, fixtures, equipment (FF&E) you use to do business. Feel free to modify the WBS to be sure to capture all of your overhead elements so that the total dollars used to support your departments adds up to the total corporate overhead rate necessary to be recovered against the business volume you are doing.

Having done this, ask yourself the hard questions for each expenditure –

- What function does the expenditure perform?
- Is that level of expenditure really necessary to produce expected sales?
- Is the increase in price caused by that expenditure worth the decrease in value to the customer?
- If the function is essential, can it be achieved in another manner at lower cost?

Most companies in general strive to reduce overhead. So what does VA offer them? Why focus on VA? VA doesn't perform magic in reducing overhead. Its real benefit is as a deliberate accelerator of thought – on this project, at this time, at this moment. The focus on function, the placing of cost against function is difficult but the focus stimulates obvious and not so obvious ways to reduce and/or control overhead cost.

Performing a value analysis WBS of overhead costs makes them really visible. It shines a light on them! Just think, if you can reduce overhead by 5% you can keep your product price the same and make 5% more profit. Or, you can reduce your price by 5% and make your product more valuable to the customer and more competitive in the market. This is a good way VA helps to make more money without impacting your product.

❊❊❊

Included in overhead are processes and procedures in your Company that cost you money and waste your resources. Here is an example of savings on a managerial process.[14]

A five billion dollar per year business unit of a 20+ billion dollar Fortune 500 company wanted to implement a new integrated electronic financial control system. The system, called APEX, was developed by the German Company; SAP. It integrated the total business processes including sales, order entry, production progress, requirements for flow down, and shipping and billing. It is widely used by many companies in the U.S. and Europe and by many federal agencies including some in the Department of Defense (DoD).

Because the system is so all-encompassing, there was considerable work involved in entering a new contract award into the system. One reason for the delay was the large amount of effort to enter all the required data including contract type, unit price, quantity, delivery, quality and other contract requirements, and billing and shipping information. With the APEX system, this information is typically entered into the system before a contract

---

14 Contributed by James R. Vickers, AVS, Corporate Value Manager

is "released." A contract must be released before a charge account can be opened and change numbers issued so work can begin.

Because of the requirements to input, interpret, and check the data before work starts, there was a six to eight week delay from the time a contract award was received until work could begin. In contrast, before APEX, work was started within one to two weeks from award receipt. This caused great concern with the performing organization because they would start work with a built-in two months schedule delay.

The problem was so great that the President of the Business Unit dictated that a value team be formed to investigate and resolve the problem. One thing that also led to her doing so, instead of just letting those involved try to work it out, was the fact that another business unit; the first to implement APEX, was having even greater delays and not working efficiently.

A VA team was formed under the joint leaders of the Comptroller who represented all the financial interests, and the director of contract support who represented the programs and operations as well as contracts. Subject matter experts were called in from each of the disciplines involved including shipping, subcontracts, production, and billing and order entry. It was the latter who had the most responsibility inputting the data and getting the system working.

The first action the team took was to map the process. They found that there were 24 individual points, each requiring a decision, action, and/or input, and usually an approval. Efforts were undertaken to speed up this process by locating the data entry personnel in the program office near the people who would provide them decisions on what to input (for example – what the quantity of the contract really meant and how to display it in APEX). The team's efforts at moving data entry personnel into the program areas and providing better guidance on how to interpret a contract resulted in the total time being reduced to a little over three weeks. This brought the time to release a contract down to less than six weeks, but still there was a long way to go.

The second step was to do a function analysis of each of the steps in the process and to determine in total what was required and when it was required. It was found that although all the steps were required, many were not needed until considerably later in the life of the contract. For example, shipping information was not required until you were going to ship, which was often after a year or two.

Further study concentrated on what was actually necessary to release a contract to begin work. It revealed that only four pieces of data were required by APEX for an initial release – the contract number, the customer name and address, the program manager and the DPAS Code (the Defense Priority Code to see if it was a DoD rated order). These four pieces of data were called the "shell" of the contract. With this information work could begin and charge numbers were now released.

Once charge numbers were released, program management could refine inputs on quantities to be delivered, and then provide quality requirements and production orders to the manufacturing department. Including the DPAS code and contract number allowed subcontracts to be issued (often times they already had the quantity from their quote upon which the original bid was based).

The team adapted the process of shelling a contract, and the time needed from contract award to the first release of work shrank from over six weeks to less than 4 days. Of course the remainder of the contract requirements still had to be filled in, but it was easier since the pressure to "get the contract in the system so they can start work" was gone. The result was declared a major success by the president.

A major lesson learned was the importance of function analysis. Specifically identifying the basic function of the objective (**release work**) and finding what supporting functions were required. Additionally, the time when each function needed to be performed was studied and proved to be the key to success (since no functions were removed in the end, only some were performed earlier).

The secret message in this –

You can reduce your expenses, reduce your price, become more competitive and make more money using value analysis.

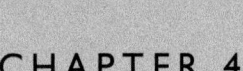

CHAPTER 4

Making it up in volume!

If you don't fix your revenue or expenses to be in sync, this a surely a good way to go broke!

"We'll make it up in volume" is the classic line I've heard time and again from, for example, a businessman who is selling a few widgets for $0.90 cents each, a price just below the $1.00 cost to manufacture them and losing money on every one of them! Somehow he thinks that if he can sell millions of them (make it up in volume) he will be better off. No, he won't. He'll just continue to lose the money he puts into the endeavor unless he analyzes why he is losing and changes his business model.

What often occurs is that the allocation of the fixed cost component is too high over the first few widgets and not fully distributed over the entire volume of production run over the life of the equipment. Why burden the first few widgets with all the tooling cost and set-up cost to get started?

Another excuse I hear for the problem is that the business is low on the "learning curve" or the "experience curve," and as soon as that improves, productivity will make up for the losses. This is only partially true. Everyone knows that the cost to manufacture the first widget is not as efficient as the last widget.

There could be a myriad of reasons that expenses are more than revenue. However, just increasing volume doesn't guarantee profit.

※※※

Break-even analysis is a method used in value analysis to determine the quantity at which the total costs of two proposals are equal, and beyond which one proposal becomes less expensive than the other. It is also used by economists and others for determining the quantity of a product that must be sold to make the product or service profitable. Jerry Kaufman, in his text,[15] indicates that break-even refers to that point where the revenues received equal the invested expenses to generate those revenues. His text is a must read for those who wish to delve deeper into the various types and graphing of experience curves and break-even distributions.

In performing VA during product development, break-even analysis can be used before implementation begins, to determine the level of service of each system that needs to be achieved before one proposal becomes more expensive than the other.

Break-even analysis can also be used after implementation begins, to determine whether it would be economical to implement a proposal to perform additional service, or implement a change on the remaining quantity of service to be provided.

Break-even analysis studies the relationship between fixed costs and variable costs. The break-even point is the point at which the total costs of two proposals are equal. Thus, by setting the total costs of each proposal equal at the break-even point, one

---

15 *Value Engineering for the Practitioner*, by J. Jerry Kaufman, North Carolina State University, College of Engineering, 1990, 3rd edition, pg 7-11.

can solve the equation. The following symbols are used to derive the break-even point equation:

F_1 = Fixed cost of proposal 1
V_1 = Variable cost of proposal 1
F_2 = Fixed cost of proposal 2
V_2 = Variable cost of proposal 2
X = Break-even. Or cross-over point in terms of quantity (number of units)

At the Break-even Point:

$$F_1 + V_1(X) = F_2 + V_2(X)$$

$$(V_1 - V_2)X = F_2 - F_1$$

$$X = \frac{F_2 - F_1}{V_1 - V_2} \quad \text{(Before the Fact Equation)}$$

Once implementation has begun, an "after the fact" break-even equation can be produced by letting F_1 be the zero. The fixed costs of proposal 1 must be considered spent for the first few quantities completed, so one cannot now consider fixed costs against proposal 1.

To implement proposal 2 will require a new expenditure of funds for fixed costs. Hence, the equation becomes:

$$X = \frac{F_2}{V_1 - V_2}$$

The following example illustrates the method of calculating the break-even point:

Proposal 1 is to produce an item costing $50 each with a fixed cost for development and implementation of $50,000.

Proposal 2 is to produce the same item at a cost of $45 each with a fixed cost of $125,000 for development and implementation.

Calculate the number of items necessary to be produced for proposal 2 to become cost effective using the break-even equation:

$$\frac{\$125,000 - \$50,000}{\$50 - \$45} = \frac{\$75.000}{\$5} = 15,000 \text{ items}$$

If proposal 1 production had already been started and proposal 2 was to be considered (that is, modify the production by introducing new equipment) then the following additional items would need to be produced to be economical:

$$\frac{\$125,000}{\$50 - \$45} = 25,000 \text{ items}$$

This answer assumes that the fixed costs for proposal 1 had been incurred, but that none of the variable cost had been expended. In performing work, one can often save variable cost by stopping work. If, however, one cannot save the exact variable dollars shutting down the work, it is proper to add the sunk variable cost (now a fixed cost) to the fixed cost of proposal 2.

Similarly, some of the fixed cost of proposal 1 may be recouped through resale of the equipment, thereby reducing the fixed cost of proposal 2.

To make more money it is now up to marketing to see if predicted sales will support the proposed change and added investment.

Jerry Kaufman[16] goes on to state that "In commercial and industrial markets, the annual production quantity is a business objective. Once established, this sales goal represents the basis for the type of tooling used, the amount of capital to be invested, market share, profit, and all the other financial relationships which pivot about the product itself."

The secret message in this –

You can provide better value, sell more, and make more money using value analysis.

---

16 ibid

CHAPTER 5

Are sunk costs holding you back?

*The past is past – look only to the present and
the future for success.*

The challenge of change is the hiccup to success. Most people resist change because it is more comfortable doing it the old way than trying a new way. That is human nature. Cost becomes secondary to their thinking until realizing that they are denying different business opportunities and methods by not learning how to take them on.

For example, I've seen many clients rush to hire engineers that specialize in concrete design and construction just to start design work. In doing this, they have in effect, created sunk cost by ruling out designs using alternative materials. Had they performed a value analysis of the structural system they might have found that steel was more economical before design work began.

Sometimes owners use the selected concrete designer to conduct an economic analysis of the right structural system to use. You can guess that concrete would come out on top. You have no idea what it would take to have a concrete designer change to steel design and, if that happened, you might have the most costly steel design available.

To make that change, rather than changing the individual, one would be better off using a design firm experienced in steel design.

***

You might have the same reaction from a mouse trap manufacturer who sold his product to **catch mice** and **kill mice.** Suppose you asked him to stop making mouse traps and produce something that would **eliminate mice** so they wouldn't come around in the first place. The mouse trap user (home owner) would probably rather have a product to eliminate mice than to have to trap and kill them and then have to pick up the dead bodies and dispose of them.

With the manufacture's sunk investment in his factory, production equipment, and supplier chain you could expect him to resist going out of the mouse trap manufacturing business even if producing a different product were more profitable. It is human nature to let habits, attitudes, and sunk cost hold you back. That is no way to make more money.

***

You think that it can't happen? This is what happened to Eastman Kodak. It was a company that was very successful in the past, but ignored the paradigm change to digital cameras because it made most of its revenues and "money" on film and film processing. The basic consumer function they provided was **display image** using film and paper. They made an incredible 70-80% profit margin on film and processing, all of which vanished. Now their stock[17] sits in the tank at $0.11 cents per share down from $27.00 a share just 6 years ago and a high of $95.00 some 20 years ago.

---

17 The internet, Finance.Yahoo.com, EKDKQ stock report chart.

Eastman Kodak (EKDKQ)

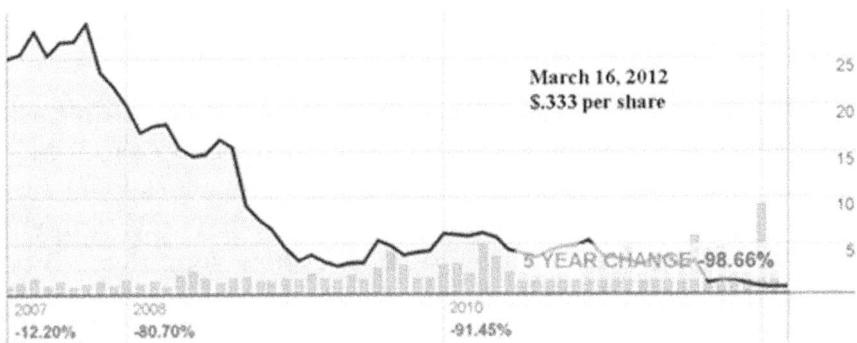

As reported by the news,[18] they were warned long before this happened by their own employees, but were too entrenched to believe it and create change to adopt to new technology.

In 1976, a 25 year old employee filed a patent for a new invention he called electronic "filmless photography." He called it this because the word "digital" in the 1970's carried a bad reputation. It was viewed as experimental, expensive, esoteric, and unreliable. That's why he called it electronic when he presented it to the company Board. It was a bold title for a presentation about a new technology that didn't use anything Kodak had spent 100 years developing to that point. Also, there was the simple fact that he was presenting it to "film guys."

He had figured out a way to **display image** without using film or prints. During the meeting one executive took a check out of his wallet and slammed it down on the table challenging the employee to "take a picture of that!" He did, and instantly it was displayed on a TV screen in the room. Quickly, negativity filled the room:

- It didn't have enough resolution.
- It didn't match the quality of Kodachrome prints.

18 MSN, July 31, 2013, Rochester, NY (The Street)

- The camera didn't fit into Kodak's vertically integrated business system.
- Even though Kodak was a small city in the 1970's, it didn't have the infrastructure to manufacture digital cameras.

What struck the presenter was that the executives didn't ask about the technology. They didn't ask how the device that captures the image and reads it out electronically worked. They didn't ask how he got the storage to work or what kind of memory was used. All they wanted to know is how soon it could be developed to market as a consumer product.

Even in the 1980's and 1990's when the electronic engineering group needed a camera to continue tinkering with digital photography they got no support. They would leave the plant, drive down the street and buy a Canon camera at the local electronics shop.

Kodak had a three decade opportunity to overcome its resistance to change on how they **displayed image** to the consumer, but that would be a product that bypassed the need for film – the company's lifeblood, a lucrative business that once controlled 90% of the rolled-film market. To them, the acceptance of change was suicide.

Now they are trying to salvage some money by selling off their sunk cost assets.

✳✳✳

In a paper written by Gary Meyers,[19] prior expenditures, known as sunk costs, are customarily excluded from economic analyses in support of decision-making. This practice appears to date back at least to the beginning of engineering economics and perhaps farther into the past. Arthur Mellon Wellington, whom many

---

19 SAVE conference paper, 2005, *Money from an Intuitive Perspective: Another Application of Function Analysis and FAST to Understand Decision-Making in Practice*, Gary R. Myers, PE,_CVS®, SAVE International Knowledge Bank, web site – http://www.value-eng.org/knowledge_bank/

recognize as the father of engineering economics, implied the exclusion of past expenditures when stressing in the late 1800's that any decision that increases costs must be profitable in and of itself.[20]

In the 1930's, when Eugene Grant first published his Principles of Engineering Economy,[21] the practice of ignoring sunk costs seems to have been well established. As Grant states, "A sunk cost is a past expenditure or an obligation already incurred, which must be ignored as having nothing to do with a choice between two alternatives for the future."

The practice continues today. For example, modern value practitioners echo Grant's advice: "Only costs expected to be incurred during the life cycle of the analysis (after the present time) are included in the cost estimates of alternatives. Therefore, sunk costs have no direct bearing on the results of the LCCA [life cycle cost analysis], since the asset or benefit provided is available regardless of which alternative is selected."[22]

This practice is founded on the principle that only those expenditures and receipts that can occur in the future are under the control of the decision-maker. A past expenditure is simply one of the actions that resulted in the situation existing in the present time. Of course, past expenditures may indirectly contribute to a future expenditure or receipt, such as when an already purchased piece of equipment can be salvaged if a particular alternative is implemented. In this example, however, it is the prospect of a future salvage value that is relevant to the current decision, not the past expenditure itself. The fact that someone can't change the past and undo the past expenditure seems to be an objective and reasonable basis for this practice.

Unfortunately, individuals often don't follow this rule in their everyday decision-making. This being the case, they may

---

20 Arthur Mellon Wellington; The Economic Theory of Railway Location; John Wiley and Sons/Engineering News; New York; 1887, pg 15.

21 Eugene L. Grant; *Principles of Engineering Economy*; The Ronald Press Company; New York; 1938, pg 179.

22 Stephen J. Kirk and Alphonse Dell'Isola; *Life Cycle Costing for Design Professionals*, McGraw-Hill, Inc., 1995, pg 33.

not always practice it in their business activities, even when aware of it and espousing agreement with the rationale behind it. As shown by numerous experiments, individuals routinely do consider sunk costs when making decisions.

For example, one experiment showed a definite correlation between the price an individual paid for a theater ticket and that same individual's probability of actually attending the event at some time in the future.[23] Another well-known experiment shows that those individuals who had paid for a ticket to a basketball game were more likely to brave a blizzard to attend the game than were those who had received the ticket as a gift.[24] The conclusion that individuals often don't follow this objective and reasonable rule is known as the "sunk cost effect," or even the "sunk cost fallacy."

❊❊❊

I remember when I was involved in the renovation of a large Government office building and the contract required sheet metal air conditioning duct work to be installed throughout the building. The prime contractor had a value engineering (VE) incentive clause in his contract and wanted to offer a value engineering change proposal to change the metal duct system to fiber duct and meet the same air flow requirements. The change would save about $150,000 and the prime contractor would share the savings 50/50 with the Government.

The mechanical subcontractor, however, wouldn't cooperate. He had recently purchased a sheet metal forming machine for about $100,000. He said he needed a return-on-investment on the equipment and told us he had to use it to offset its capital cost or he'd lose money.

I told him to forget the machine. It was sunk cost. He could make more money right away installing the fiber duct on our

---

23 Hal R. Arkes and Catherine Blumer, *The Psychology of Sunk Cost*, The Journal of Organizational Behavior and Decision Making; 1985, pgs 127-128

24 Richard Thaler; "Toward a Positive Theory of Consumer Choice;" The Journal of Economic Behavior and Organization; 1980, pg 47.

job. He would get paid for his fiber duct work with its normal overhead and profit, plus he would split the savings with the prime contractor and walk away with an additional $37,500 in VE profits for work he didn't have to do.

If he was smart he would junk the sheet metal forming machine and do all the fiber duct work that he could on future jobs, but he was stubborn. He couldn't get past the fact that he had made an investment that wouldn't be used on his first job. He forgot that his first function was to **make money** for his business and not worry about past spending on the equipment purchase as long as he came out ahead.

The owner loved the change from steel to fiber duct. He was only interested in getting the required air flow in each room at any lower cost that could be achieved which was one-half of the total savings. The story ended when the prime contractor terminated his metal duct contract and hired another subcontractor to provide the fiber duct work.

✻✻✻

Significant capital expenditures and large down payments should not be expected to be amortized over the life of the first job or first year. If you plan to stay in business, this type of equipment should be depreciated over its useful life span say – a 10 or 15 year period as a part of fixed overhead.

And to hedge your risk in investing in a change, see if you can phase in capital expenditures over a longer period of time while you are testing market reaction. Then you can decide whether or not to ramp up production.

✻✻✻

During development of the Phoenix missile at the Naval Air Systems Command, a value engineering (VE) improvement program was employed in the procurement contract to reduce the per missile cost. Knowing in advance that value engineering ideas would be generated that would result in changes to the missile, we were given six designated missiles during the production run to "play" with and incorporate VE ideas.

These designated missiles enabled the company to modify them to test out approved ideas without interrupting the production run. Once the ideas were tested to prove that required performance of the missiles was not degraded, the ideas were incorporated in future production runs substantially lowering the unit cost of each missile.

Avoiding delays in production runs in this fashion helped keep production cost down and enabled the manufacturer to make more money than if he had been required to stop and restart his production line.

✳✳✳

This is similar to another VE feat told by the Manager of a Ford Motor Company dealership in Louisiana. They did a study of the transmission of a new car and saw that they could remove more than a dozen parts (pieces of the transmission) with no apparent loss of performance.

The Manager went to Detroit to make a presentation of his VE ideas in the Board room. The executives in the room were apparently astounded and said it couldn't be done, that the car wouldn't work. At that point, the Manager pulled the pieces of a transmission out of his bag and placed them on the conference room table.

He said, "Look out the window at my car. I drove it all the way up from Louisiana without those parts in it and it worked just fine!"

The moral of the story – give the man a car to test VE ideas on. Don't make him use his own car. It's good for business and good for making more money!

The secret message in this –

You can forget costly past expenses by looking forward toward the future and doing what is necessary to make the future profitable using value analysis.

CHAPTER 6

Ownership costs

The act of ownership is the user determining value.

The more you want a user to want something, to own something, the more your sales will increase, and you'll be making the money you seek. Remember, however, the value of something to a user is more than just the price of it. It has to work for as long as the user needs it. It has to have dependability, timeliness, and reliability with meantime between failure (MTBF) that is acceptable. It has to have easy maintainability, reasonable operating cost, and good trade-in or salvage value. That, in a nutshell, expresses the elements of the quality of a product or service.

Carlos Fallon wrote[25] that price, plus the costs of ownership, operation, maintenance, and disposal constitute the elements of cost to the customer. All such elements of cost affect the competitive position of a product.

---

25 *Value Analysis, 2ⁿᵈ revised edition,* Carlos Fallon, The Miles Value Foundation, 1980, pg 22

The total cost of ownership or life cycle cost (LCC) is the economic measure of value. Therefore when the customer has choices on how to achieve a function at a required performance level, the lowest LCC choice represents the best value at that point in time. If marketed properly to the customer, that choice is the one that should sell and bring income to the business.

A value analysis (VA) choice, when judged on equivalent LCC, is the best hope to provide better value without sacrifice of required quality or performance. That is much better than what simple cost reduction offers which implies sacrifice of something desired.

***

The value of a system or service includes consideration of what it costs to acquire it, to use it, and the cost of performance to the user for as long as it is needed. Therefore, a good measure of value is to calculate the user's total cost.

Cost of repair, operations, preventive maintenance, logistic support, utilities, depreciation and replacement, in addition to capital cost, all reflect the total value of a product to a user. Calculation of LCC for each function alternative is a way to judge whether required quality is being maintained in sufficient degree to prevent undue degradation of reliability, performance, and maintainability.

The concept of economic analysis used in LCC, requires that comparisons be made between things that are similar in nature; i.e., a comparison of apples and apples. For example, one cannot compare the LCC of a bus to a car, nor can one compare a house to a school on an equal basis.

However, all ideas can be compared on a LCC basis if all alternatives were defined to satisfy the same basic function or set of functions. In addition to comparable functions, economic analysis requires that one consider alternative choices on the same:

- time frame
- quantities

- quality
- levels of service
- economic conditions
- market conditions
- operating conditions

Life cycle cost analysis requires the knowledge of several economic concepts. One of these is the concept of equivalent costs to deal with time frame. Equivalent costs are typically developed by equating all costs to a common date (base year) using an interest rate to adjust for variable expenditure years. You must also hold the economic conditions constant while the cost consequences of each alternative are being developed. That is, the same economic factors are applied to each alternative using a uniform methodology.

Following, is a generic chart of cost elements frequently associated with the LCC of products or services.

Life Cycle Cost Elements		
Initial Costs	**Operation Costs**	**Other Costs**
Design	Labor	Financing
Manufacturing	Utilities	Insurance
Shipping	Maintenance	Taxes
Procurement	Repair	Permits
Overhead	Alteration	Salvage
Storage	Replacement	
Sales		

The above chart does not contain all the detail LCC elements for every product because some costs are peculiar to specific products. Design cost might include market surveys, research, pilot production and testing. Manufacturing cost would include all costs from raw materials to tooling, setup, production and labor.

For example, to consider the LCC of an automobile one would have to include the cost of title and license under other costs. Life cycle costing includes all costs, from "cradle to grave" of a system and its use, upkeep, and final disposition.

✳✳✳

The first task one must accomplish in performing a LCC analysis is to determine the period of time for which the analysis of accumulated costs is to occur. What is the life span of a system or service?

The lease term or the intended service life is used most often. Other methods include the depreciation period allowed for tax computation, mortgage or financing period, or the length of contract when applicable.

One difficulty in determining life span is the realization that individual life spans or usefulness of systems or components of a product or service may be quite different. For example, the life of a car engine may be 150,000 miles, whereas the life of the tires may be only 40,000 miles.

In performing a value study, the life span selected should be the period of time that the owner or user needs the system or service. User need determines life span when judging life cycle cost and worth and when comparing alternatives. When the user feels that the need is perpetual, or cannot be fixed to a precise period of time, a reasonable period must be assumed using one of the above methods (tax, finance or contract period).

A second choice for determining the life span to use would be a period related to a financial decision of management, such as a contract, or loan, because life cycle costing results in a financial evaluation of alternatives. Use of a stated product design life is the weakest choice because it is determined by the seller rather than the user.

Regardless of the procedure to determine life span, there is one rule that must be followed:

Use the same life span for evaluating all choices.

Be consistent and do not compare the LCC of one item stated to last 8 years with another item stated to last 12 years on different life spans. One may use 8, 12, or even 20 years as the life spans for both items.

For the items noted, one with an estimated 8 year life and the other with an estimated 12 year life, assume that a 20 year life span is selected as the analysis. One must then calculate residual value of each item in the 20th year, which is done as follows:

1. The life cycle costs for the 8-year item would show costs for replacement of the item in the 9th and 17th years. By the 20th year the last item replaced would only be 4 years old. Hence, it would have a residual or salvage value of ½ its replacement cost in the 20th year.

2. Similarly, the 12-year item would be replaced in the 13th year. In the 20th year, that item would have used 8 years of its 12 year service life and have a residual value of 1/3 its replacement cost in the 20th year.

Use of residual value helps compare "apples to apples." The above example assumes uniform depreciation.

❊❊❊

The easiest estimating methodology to use is to compute the present value of all alternatives using the constant dollar approach. Using this approach, one estimates all costs based on the present year. One ignores inflation in estimating cost to be incurred in later years. Inflation is considered through application of the discount rate used to convert future year costs to present worth costs.

One discount rate is easier to use (and probably more accurate) than trying to guess both inflation and interest rate which may change from year to year. The discount rate is the difference between inflation and interest. The U.S. Office of Management & Budget bases all of its economic analysis on a discount rate of 7 percent and has done so for the past 30 years.

Replacement cost for a component of the item in a future year is calculated based on the cost to perform the work in the current year. One asks, "If I had to replace it now, instead of ~ years from now, what would it cost?"

The following is an example for calculating LCC costs for the **transport people** function (assume four people) by evaluating the business decision to purchase a car or rent one for a 5 year rental period. You may need a car longer, but the rental period is the maximum commonly offered in the market so both cars have to be judged on the same life span.

In the present worth approach, the equivalent cost baseline is today's values. All replacement and annual costs are calculated as though they were to occur today. This example uses the LCC Value Technology Template[26] that automatically does the math.

In the first section of the template you list the first cost or initial cost for each alternate. In the case shown this would be the cost to purchase the car or the initial deposit on renting a car.

In the middle section of the template you itemize the replacement costs that occur, and the year they probably will occur, for each idea during the life span.

In the third or bottom section of the template you list the annual recurring costs for each alternate. In addition to annual costs for registration, fuel and maintenance for each you will have the unique monthly rental cost (converted to an annual cost) for the rental alternate.

---

26 SAVE International sells the author's Technology Templates on their web site at: http://www.value-eng.org/education_publications_bookstore. php#3

Not shown in this analysis is any interest on the loan to purchase the car or the collateral benefit of the tax deduction that the business owner could get if the rented car is used for business purposes.

LIFE CYCLE COST

Description:				Original Idea		Alternate #1	
Project Life Cycle = 5 Years				Purchase Car		Rent Car	
Discount Rate = 7.00%							
Present Time = Date of Use							
INITIAL COSTS	Quantity	UM	Unit Price	Est.	PW	Est.	PW
Purchase car	1	EA	$30,000	30,000	30,000		0
Rental deposit	1	EA	$2,000		0	2,000	2,000
					0		0
					0		0
Total Initial Cost					$ 30,000		$ 2,000
Initial Cost PW Savings (Compared to Original Design)							$ 28,000
REPLACEMENT COST/ SALVAGE VALUE							
Description		Year	PW Factor				
New Tires		4	0.7629	450	343	450	343
Trade-in Value		5	0.7130	(10,000)	(7,129)	0	0
Total Replacement/Salvage Costs					$ (6,786)		$ 343
ANNUAL COSTS							
Description		Escl. %	PWA				
Personal Property Tax		0.0%	4.100	1,200	4,920	0	0
License Registration		0.0%	4.100	35	144	35	144
Maintenance		0.0%	4.100	500	2,050	500	2,050
Gasoline - assume same mpg		0.0%	4.100	1,000	4,100	1,000	4,100
Lease Rental $400/month		0.0%	4.100	0	0	4,800	19,681
Total Annual Costs (Present Worth)					$ 11,214		$ 25,975
Total Life Cycle Costs (Present Worth)					$ 34,428		$ 28,318
Life Cycle Savings (Compared to Original Idea)							$ 6,110
			Periodic Payment Factor				
Total Life Cycle Costs (Annualized)			0.2439	$ 8,397	Per Year	$ 6,906	Per Year

✳✳✳

In this day and age of climate change and environmental problems businesses have found that they can make more money by addressing the LCC value of their products. Consumers will purchase value if they can be shown that their overall costs will be lower if the life cycle of their use is anticipated to be reasonably right. That is causing manufacturers to develop "green" products – mainly in cars and lighting at the moment.

Selecting change based on the lowest LCC choice supports the claim that VA does not negatively impact quality. Product quality has no direct relationship to product cost! It is not absolutely true that the more something costs means that it has higher quality. You can have a high quality Chevy and a low quality Cadillac or vice versa.

Product quality is, however, directly related to performance. If a thing works as it is designed to do, lasts as long as it is claimed to last, fails when it is predicted to fail, can be maintained at the cost and frequency stated, and has the end-of-life residual value expected – then the product is of the highest quality possible!

LCC is the economic tool used by value analysts to quantify all those performance issues in terms of money so products performing the same function can be compared.

The secret message in this -

You can increase sales and make more money by anticipating product use by the customer and make your products more valuable to them over their life time.

CHAPTER 7

Getting more out of contracts

Once you have been awarded a contract you have all their money! All you have to do to get it is perform.

If you are the low bidder on a contract, and it is awarded to you, the first thing you should do is recheck your bid to see that you can perform it for the price you offered and still make money. If you think that you might have trouble obtaining the materials needed, components are out of stock, the labor skills required become unavailable, or that your margins of profit are really too low to be sustainable – then value analysis is the tool you need to reduce these risks.

Trying to make up a potential loss position with change orders is counter productive to fostering and sustaining good human relations with your client. You want to be considered for future contract work. Troublemakers are remembered, and submitting changes to make more money is not good marketing. However, suggesting a change that saves both parties money and still meets client performance is a win-win situation. This is true whether or not you have a value engineering incentive clause (VEIC) in your contract.

※※※

The Federal government, however, has a specific special deal. Under their Federal Acquisition Regulation (FAR 52.248-1) they provide for the inclusion of a VEIC in Federal contracts. This allows you to submit value engineering change proposals (VECP's) to your contracting officer to save money for the government and increase your profit on the contract by sharing in the instant savings, collateral benefits, and sometimes royalties.

If you don't have a VEIC in your government contract just ask for it. The clause is free, and there is no reason your contracting officer should not give it to you. In fact if it was left out of the contract because the contracting officer deemed there was no potential to save money then, the very act of requesting the clause proves that judgment wrong.

There are two important rules in participating in the FAR VECP program:

1. You **must** have the clause in your contract **before** you submit a VECP. When you do submit a VECP you **must** identify it as such at the time of submittal or you might lose your share of the benefits.
2. You **must,** at the time of first submittal, indentify the specific requirement in the contract you propose to change. Point to it by specific reference to its page and item number or drawing and section number.

※※※

Have you ever been awarded a contract for construction, leasing, supplies or services and, after reading all of its requirements,

46

thought to yourself that what they were asking for could be done better, cheaper, or faster if they let you do it your way?

Contract requirements are full of specifications for required materials, performance, testing, packaging, delivery, installation, and maintenance. For government procurement these specifications are often generic enough in nature, so that they cover other company's products in order to be competitive.

In fact, the first reason to submit a VECP is if you have a proprietary product that could not have been specified by the Government under competitive procurement laws. Manufacturers of proprietary products can get their product on the job by offering it as a VECP through the trade subcontractor or general prime contractor provided they can show a life-cycle cost benefit to the client by accepting it.

That was how the Trane Corporation got its new, first generation, energy efficient chiller on a major government building project. Their new chiller was not included in the Federal specification for chillers, so contractors did not include it in their bidding. The new chiller cost a little more at the time, but over the life-cycle it saved a great deal of energy cost that offset the initial cost increase.

For a few years, until the Federal specification caught up and competition caught on, Trane could then keep offering their new chiller on every government project where a chiller was needed. That's a good way to break into the business with a new innovation!

✳✳✳

There are some risks in participating in a contract VE program. You are being asked to invest your resources in developing and submitting proposals. You will lose this investment every time a VECP is disapproved. In addition, you cannot delay performance under your contract while your proposal is being processed.

You can minimize your risk, but not avoid it. Submit good VECP's with adequate data the first time, and do it early in the contract. Discuss your idea with the client before investing in a major effort to prepare a proposal. Divulgence of your idea will not jeopardize your right to a fair share of the savings. However, when you do discuss your idea with others in advance of submittal, follow those discussions with a letter of intent to submit a VECP then all will know you are taking action. Here are the general ingredients for a VECP proposal:

Format – No special forms are required. Use your company letterhead and estimating forms. Don't forget to identify it as a VECP.

Your Idea – Describe both the old way and your idea. Give advantages and disadvantages of each.

Supporting Data – Subcontractor and vendor transmittals, manufacturers literature, shop drawings, calculations, brochures, test data, certifications, and samples are the type of data desired to make your proposal complete.

Costs – Provide separate cost estimates for the old way and your idea. The difference between these estimates will be shared or, if the new idea costs more you will receive the difference in a change order. Remember, overhead, profit, and bond need not be included in either estimate. That money need not be shared – that's another benefit.

Collateral – Give your best judgment on the effect your idea will have on future ownership costs to the client. You will normally share in the average first year savings.

Contract Changes – Identify each requirement in the contract you want changed, and tell how to do it. Indicate the effect, if any, your idea will have on the rest of the unchanged work in the contract.

Time – State what impact your idea will have on time for completion, delivery or occupancy. Indicate how long your offer is good.

Remember you are continuing to perform on the contract while review of the proposal is on-going.

Previous Submittals – Indicate if your idea has been approved before, under another contract. This is a selling point in your favor.

Copies – An original and five copies is recommended, so that the client can have the proposal reviewed concurrently to expedite a reply.

Submit your proposal as you would any other change order or invoice – to your contracting officer or authorized representative if one has been designated for your contract.

❋❋❋

The following is a VECP example for submittal by a Contractor to the Government at the start of construction. It involves changing its lighting system from fluorescent to LED (light emitting diode). It is based on a typical Government Office Headquarters building, 5-story, with a gross area of 283,547 square feet and a typical mix of space types. This VECP increases initial cost, but has a large amount of life-cycle savings over a 15 year period. The 15 year term was selected for illustratation because that is normally the maximum length the Government will fix a term for a lease from a developer owner and is reasonable enough to be below the 20-year prospectus authorization limit.

The new way to **"create contrast"** in office space with equivalent lumens is the use of LED light fixtures to replace fluorescent light fixtures. The amount of contrast created by lighting depends upon the lighting design and the intensity of the lighting in the space. What LED does offer is equivalent light levels for lower energy consumption. Therefore, this example is based on replacing the designed 2x4 fixtures (3 tube, T-8 lamps, 100 watt fixture) on a one for one basis with a LED 40 watt fixture of an equivalent light level.

The LED fixtures have a 50,000 hour lamp life compared to the fluorescent lamp life of 20,000 hours. To consider the impact of these lamp hours you need to know that the total number of hours in a year, based on 24 x 365, is 8,760 hours. In an office application, the lighting would be expected to be used 250 days a year (not counting holidays and weekends) for 12 hours a day, or 3,000 hours a year.

Typical T8 linear fluorescent lamps have an operating life of around 20,000 hours. Normal group re-lamping cycles associated with this product typically occur at between 60% and 70% of rated life. Therefore, a T8 lamp would be group re-lamped at about 13,000 hours of operation (65% of 20,000 hours). Based on 3,000 operating hours per year, group re-lamping would occur in year 5 of operation.

The electrical contractor on the job needs to indicate that he will replace all 2x4 fluorescent fixtures with 2x4 LED fixtures and compute the new lighting loads.

The chart below illustrates one way to calculate the block load of lighting and power for a building. It shows a side by side comparison the fluorescent lighting and LED lighting. The power section (for outlets in the office) is in the center of the chart and is unchanged for either lighting system. This chart is needed to calculate the difference in incoming amperage to the building because the LED lighting system uses less panels and breakers because of the reduced electric current the system draws.

From these computations it can be seen that even though the number of fixtures has not changed, the incoming electrical service is reduced from 6,000 amps to 5,400 amps or 10%. That means the same number of lighting fixtures can be installed with fewer lighting panels and breakers because more lights can now be on the same circuit.

The following load comparison was validated by Cree,[27] a leading manufacturer and supplier of LED fixtures. To be conservative the lighting loads for the LED system were calculated at 50% of the fluorescent system even though the actual equiva-

---

27 Bob Roller, VP, Business Development, Cree.

lency is 40%. Also, the percentage of spare power capacity for lighting was calculated the same for both systems.

Electrical Block Load Computation

Project: Office Headquarters Building
Lighting System Comparison

PROGRAM AREA	NSF	FLUORESCENT SYSTEM			POWER		LED SYSTEM		
		LIGHTING WATTS/SF	CONNECTED KW	NUMBER FIXTURES	POWER WATTS/SF	CONNECTED KW	LIGHTING WATTS/SF	CONNECTED KW	NUMBER FIXTURES
Net Usable Area									
Private Office	28,000	1.5	42.0	280	0.5	56.0	0.75	21.0	280
Open Office	65,000	1.5	97.5	650	1.0	162.5	0.75	48.8	650
Agency Suites	45,000	1.5	67.5	450	0.5	90.0	0.75	33.8	450
Conference	9,900	1.5	14.9	99	0.5	19.8	0.75	7.4	99
Library	1,700	1.5	2.6	17	0.5	3.4	0.75	1.3	17
Computer Room	14,000	2.0	28.0	140	8.0	110.0	1.00	14.0	140
Computer Lab/Testing	4,500	2.0	9.0	45	1.0	13.5	0.75	3.4	45
Storage Space	10,500	1.0	10.5	105	0.5	15.8	0.75	7.9	105
Training Space	7,300	1.5	11.0	73	0.5	14.6	0.75	5.5	73
Cafeteria	3,800	2.0	7.6	38	4.0	22.8	0.75	2.9	38
Auditorium	3,500	1.0	3.5	35	0.5	5.3	1.75	6.1	35
Coffee Bars	750	1.5	1.1	8	0.5	1.5	0.75	0.6	8
Fax/Printer/Copy Rooms	2,000	1.5	3.0	20	1.0	5.0	0.75	1.5	20
Loading Dock	2,200	1.5	3.3	22	0.5	4.4	0.75	1.7	22
Health Center	1,200	1.5	1.8	12	0.5	2.4	0.75	0.9	12
Security Control Center	500	1.5	0.8	5	0.5	1.0	0.75	0.4	5
Smoking Room	1,000	1.0	1.0	10	0.5	1.5	0.75	0.8	10
Vending/Break Room	3,000	1.0	3.0	30	0.5	4.5	0.75	2.3	30
Parking - interior	9,000	0.2	1.8	90	0.2	3.6	0.50	4.5	90
Subtotals	212,850		310	2,129		567.5		164.4	2,129
Gross Area	283,549								
Support Area	70,699								
Horiz Circulation 35%	24,745	1.0	24.7	247	0.5	3.2	0.50	12.4	247
Vert. Circulation 8%	5,656	1.0	5.7	57	0.5	37.1	0.50	2.8	57
Mechanical/Electrical 23%	16,261	0.5	8.1	163	1.0	8.5	0.25	4.1	163
Toilets 5%	3,535	1.0	3.5	35	0.5	24.4	0.50	1.8	35
Custodial 7%	4,949	0.5	2.5	49	0.5	3.5	0.25	1.2	49
Construction 22%	15,554								
HVAC 747 Tons					2.0	1,494.0			
HVAC VAV boxes	242,734				0.5	121.4			
Elevators	242,734				1.0	242.7			
Fire Pumps 35 Hp					1.1	38.5			
Space Capacity	274,549	0.5	137.3		1.0	411.8	0.25	68.6	
Parking, roads	399,750	0.5	199.9		0.2	279.8	0.25	99.9	
Subtotals			381.7	551		2,665.0		190.8	551.5
Total Fixtures				2,680					2,680
Subtotal KW			691.4			3,232.5		355.2	
Spare Capacity 25%			172.9			808.1		88.8	
TOTAL KW =			864.3			4,040.6		444.0	
GRAND TOTAL KW =			4,901.9					4,484.6	
For 3 phase voltage = 480 Factor = 0.83 AMPS =			5,899.6					5,391.2	
SERVICE AMPS SAY =			6,000					5,400	

The next step is to make a LCC analysis using the technology template shown in the previous Chapter.

Based on the above, fluorescent lamps need to be changed every 5 years. The estimated cost to relamp a 3-tube fixture is $5.00 each.

Their ballasts need to be changed every 7 years. The estimated cost to replace a ballast is $55.00 per fixture. The LED fixtures have no ballasts, but they do have electronic "drivers" that can fail. This is typically at a very low failure rate. There are significant savings in energy consumption. The estimated cost for electricity used in the analysis is ten-cents per kilowatt-hour.

The computations indicate that the Contractor will earn an additional $165,059 from the owner to install LED lighting (a cost increase of $0.58 per gross square foot).

The annualized savings to the owner is $48,161 per year for 15 years or a total discounted present worth savings of $438,829.

The payback period for the initial increase in expenditure based upon the annualized savings is therefore – 3.5 years. This is not bad for a 15-year life span.

LIFE CYCLE COST ANALYSIS (LCCA)

Project/Location: Sample 5 floor office building - 283,547 GSF
Item: Use LED lighting vice Flourescent

Description:					Original Design		Proposed Design	
Project Life Cycle = 15 Years					Fluorescent 2x4 Lighting		LED 2x4 Lighting	
Discount Rate = 7.00%								
Present Time = Date of Use								
INITIAL COSTS	Quantity	UM	Unit Price		Est.	PW	Est.	PW
A. Fluorescent fixtures - 2x4	2680	EA	$190		509,200	509,200		
B. LED fixtures - 2x4	2680	EA	$275				737,000	737,000
C. Lighting panels - 42 ckt	15	EA	$3,175		47,625	47,625		
D. Lighting panels - 36 ckt	10	EA	$2,700				27,000	27,000
E. Circuit breakers	446	EA	$78		34,788	34,788		
F. Circuit breakers - LED	224	EA	$78				17,472	17,472
G. Incoming service	6000	AMP	$40		240,000	240,000		
H. Incoming service - LED	5400	AMP	$40				216,000	216,000
I.								
Total Initial Cost						$ 831,613		$ 997,472
Initial Cost PW Savings (Compared to Original Design)								$ (165,859)
REPLACEMENT COST/ SALVAGE VALUE								
Description		Year	PW Factor					
A. Ballast replacement		7	0.6227		147,400	91,793		0
B. Ballast replacement		14	0.3878		147,400	57,164		0
C. Relamping fluorescent		5	0.7130		13,400	9,554		0
D. Relamping fluorescent		10	0.5083		13,400	6,811		0
E.								
Total Replacement/Salvage Costs						$ 165,322		$ -
ANNUAL COSTS								
Description		Escl. %	PWA					
A. Energy - Flourescent		0.0%	9.108		80,400	732,276		
B. Energy - LED		0.0%	9.108				32,160	292,911
D.								
E.								
Total Annual Costs (Present Worth)						$ 732,276		$ 292,911
Total Life Cycle Costs (Present Worth)						$ 1,729,211		$ 1,290,383
Life Cycle Savings (Compared to Original Design)								$ 438,829
			PP Factor					
Total Life Cycle Costs (Annualized)			0.1096	$	189,858	Per Year	$ 141,677	Per Year

PW: Present Worth
PWA: Present Worth of Annuity
PP: Periodic Payment

In addition, if the VEIC offers a standard 20% collateral savings share, the Contractor would receive a bonus reward of $9,632 for the average first year. A great way to make more money!

Our cost estimate for the LED fixtures is extremely conservative. As the LED industry grows the fixture cost is bound to come down, and the benefits will be even more magnified.

The secret message in this -

You can get your proprietary products into government work and outdo your competitors by offering value savings change proposals.

CHAPTER 8

Examining value

If it is worth less to the customer than its
price it is not good value.

The components of product value of items offered for sale depend
on the following four elements:[28]

1. Customers with money and unsatisfied wants – a market.
2. Utility to such customers – the product must suit the market.
3. Scarcity or difficulty in attainment – the product must be
   hard to get.
4. Total cost to the customer – an inverse component of value.
   Given difficulty in attainment, the customer wants to pay the
   least for overcoming that difficulty.

---

28 *Value Analysis, 2nd revised edition,* Carlos Fallon, The Miles Value Foundation,
   reprinted 1986, pg 24

Utility[29] is the quality or state of being useful or serviceable, as a farm tractor; fitness for a given purpose, as an engagement ring; aptness for a given application, as a parachute; beneficial for a given condition, as aspirin; timeliness in meeting a need, as a baby shower; suitability or convenience of location, as an oasis; in summary – completing the cycle – the capacity to satisfy wants.

The specific properties that render a product useful or esteemed are elements of utility. These properties are usually descriptive of the effectiveness with which the product performs its function. Examples are performance, quality, appearance, reliability, service and convenient delivery. The utility of each of these elements, or their combined utility, can be quantified in dollars. How? A stranded motorist quantifies utility when he says, "A gallon of gas, right now, is worth ten dollars to me!"

What does he mean by worth? Worth is an appraisal of the properties rendering a product useful or esteemed in the eyes of a person; a measure of such usefulness or esteem; the monetary equivalent of utility. It means an appraisal of the effectiveness with which a product performs its function or a system accomplishes its mission. It represents the customer's regard for the capability of a product to satisfy his wants. Carlos Fallon states[30] that "the monetary connotation of the term worth makes it possible to quantify utility in the same units as cost."

Now, in value analysis, we call the elements of utility, as elements of worth, so that we can relate them to their corresponding elements of cost.

Function is the dynamic aspect of utility. If the capacity to satisfy wants is the utility of a product; actually satisfying those wants is the function of a product. Next to value, **function** is the most important word in value analysis.

---

29 Ibid, pg 20-21
30 Ibid, pg 21

A tool in the arsenal for a business professional to judge value is the calculation of the value index (VI) for the function of the item as a whole and the function(s) of each of its major component parts or cost areas.

The VI is expressed by dividing function cost by function worth (VI = F_c / F_w). When VI = 1 - you have good value. When, for example, VI = 1.15 it indicates a 15% opportunity for value improvement if you can figure out how to do that.

Larry Miles emphasized the need for "mind tuning"[31] and "mind setting" at the beginning of a value study during the information or function phase. He discusses the importance of the team getting a "feeling" of what they are really trying to do. Miles shows tables of "Present Cost" vs "Required Cost" for functions under study.[32] From this concept, calculation of the value index began.

It is a wonderful identification technique that contributes to mind tuning the team and visually highlights the value mismatches between function cost and function worth. Those mismatches are the opportunities for value improvement, enabling management to focus on those functions that have the most potential for value improvement.

Another area to focus on are those functions with the highest magnitude of cost because changing the way one of those functions is performed may lead to the most benefits.

✷✷✷

You begin to examine the value of something by taking the whole item and breaking it down into its major components similar to a work breakdown structure (WBS). This can be done for a product, a system, a procedure, or even the components of overhead and G&A cost.

---

31 *Techniques of Value Analysis and Engineering – 3rd Edition,* Lawrence D. Miles, 1989, Lawrence D. Miles Value Foundation, pg 53.

32 Ibid, pg 48.

The following example is the WBS for a 10-inch dinner candle using the Manufacturing Value Index Technology Template[33] available from SAVE International.

In this example the first step was to list the components and cost to manufacture and ship 500,000 candles. The five components of the candle and their functions were:

Wax	**Contain Wick**
Wick	**Generate Light**
Stearic Acid	**Slow Burn Rate**
Dye	**Improve Appearance**
Scent	**Improve Odor**

Because sales were slipping the manufacturer thought he should lower production to 450,000 candles, so the second step was to introduce the proposed production volume. This 10% reduction in volume, however, did not produce a 10% reduction in total cost and had a negative impact on product unit price.

Reducing this production volume did not save in the cost of the molding equipment, number of employees, or plant overhead. It produced a value index (VI) of 1.06 representing a 6% savings of just $28,300 and a rise in required unit cost to $0.98 a candle.

The chart shown below is for a dinner candle. Think what the worth of the function would be for a birthday candle. You would need a lot less wax, no stearic acid to control the burn rate, much less wick and dye, and no scent to smell attractive.

Defining the 5 components of the candle and each of their functions, determining their cost and judging their worth, helped to identify the value mismatches and point the way to the generation of additional value for the company. It showed the team the possibilities they could achieve. A target savings potential of 11%.

---

33 SAVE International sells the author's Technology Templates on their web site at: http://www.value-eng.org/education_publications_bookstore. php#3

General
Value Index Model

PROJECT: ____10" Yellow Dinner Candle____

		PRESENT QUANTITY	500,000		PROPOSED QUANTITY	450,000		
COMPONENTS	FUNCTION	COST	COST $/each	PCT SAVINGS	WORTH	WORTH $/each	POTENTIAL SAVINGS	VALUE INDEX
Wax	Contain wick	96,750	0.19	5.0	82,721	0.18	14,029	1.17
Wick	Generate light	4,500	0.01	20.0	3,240	0.01	1,260	1.39
Stearic Acid	Slow burning	33,750	0.07	5.0	28,856	0.06	4,894	1.17
Dye	Improve appearance	20,250	0.04	5.0	17,314	0.04	2,936	1.17
Scent	Improve odor	69,950	0.14	5.0	59,807	0.13	10,143	1.17
Molding Equipment	Form shape	50,000	0.10	-10.0	49,500	0.11	500	1.01
Shrink Wrap	Encase product	2,500	0.01	99.0	23	0.00	2,478	111.11
Boxing	Package product	7,300	0.01	42.0	3,811	0.01	3,489	1.92
Labeling	Identify product	3,000	0.01	2.0	2,646	0.01	354	1.13
Manufacturing Labor	Make product	85,000	0.17	-10.0	84,150	0.19	850	1.01
Shipping	Distribute product	25,000	0.05	-3.0	23,175	0.05	1,825	1.08
Overhead	Support company	67,500	0.14	-8.0	65,610	0.15	1,890	1.03
Total Cost		465,500	0.93		420,853	0.94	44,647	1.11

Using this concept the value team speculated on reducing the circumference of the dinner candle slightly so that it would lessen the volume of the wax by 5% and not really be noticeable to the customer. This immediately reduced the amount of stearic acid, dye and scent required by 5% and affected only basic functions. It was also speculated that the wick could stop 2-inches from the bottom of a 10-inch candle and not go all the way down.

Then the impact of packaging the candles 12 to a box instead of 6 to a box, and shrink wrapped separately, was added to the analysis which affected only secondary functions, not the candle itself!

The value mismatches became readily apparent to the team as shown in the chart above. They helped establish priorities for further study, and they led the way for in-depth analysis of many more alternatives during the creative phase of the study to improve sales and profitability:

VI = 111.11 shrink wrapping
VI = 1.92 boxing
VI = 1.39 wick
VI = 1.17 wax, stearic acid, dye, scent
VI = 1.13 label
VI = 1.08 shipping

The cumulative effect of all of these initial quick ideas involving function worth had the potential to set the stage mentally for the value study team by establishing a cost savings target of $44,647, with an 11% benefit in lower cost that had only a 0.01 cent increase in unit price.

Reducing the production volume and modifying the candle design jointly brought the price to cost and profit relationship back into line. Now, if sales increase, the increased production with the lower cost to manufacture candles will be much more profitable.

This analysis was not as aggressive as it could have been. It assumed no changes to the marketability of the 10-inch dinner candle. A more aggressive study would have used marketing to seek out the Voice of the Customer (VOC). For example, to see if a 9-inch candle would be an acceptable alternative to the 10-inch size for the same use function could be studied.

VA, as you can see, has the most potential to improve business profit when it is used as a tool to invent new products within a short time-frame or to aid the design of new products "on the board" before manufacturing begins.

***

I would be remiss if I didn't mention the new target costing method, mentioned in Chapter 1, at this point because it is an excellent way to plan for and expect a consistent level of profitability now and far into the future. If one could target cost the functions of the candle well before production there would be no cost overruns because the one stringent rule of target costing is that no product target cost can be exceeded or the product will not be launched.

Following is an overview of target costing as explained by Jim Rains,[34] a leading industrial engineer and Chairman of the Miles Value Foundation:

"The main activities of comprehensive target costing are:

- Planning for target cost and target profit
- Confirmation of the target cost and profit and allocation to main portions of the product
- Assisting and promoting the activities of target cost and profit and managing them in product planning, development, design, and manufacturing preparation stages
- Achieving the target cost and profit by the activities of all areas of the business
- Evaluating target costing activities for continuous improvement.

"Target costing is not just about setting cost targets. It is an entire value chain approach to managing an enterprise. Cost targets are not budget targets. Too many managers have been taught that budgets are what you spend. Cost targets, by contrast, are something you achieve."

"Target costing is not a financial system. Typically financial systems are used by the finance department to report costs that have already been spent, rather than to manage cost expenditures before they occur."

"Target costing is not just for engineers. While engineering plays a significant role in target costing, the system requires all disciplines to be in consistent alignment with the needs of the customer.

"Target costing is not just for marketing. By the same token, if marketing does an expert effort in identifying the exact customer needs, the entire organization needs to be focused in support of those findings"

---

34 *Target Cost Management, The Ladder to Global Survival and Success,* Jim Rains, CRC Press, 2011, pg xxv.

The discipline of target costing and the development of cost tables and cost targets to achieve functions go hand-in-hand with value analysis.

The secret message in this –

You can make more money by listening to your customers and provide the functions they value and want to purchase.

CHAPTER 9

Working on the Main Idea

The main idea is expressed as the item's function. Thus, the customer could determine if the price to be paid for performing the desired function was good value. Today, we ask, "Is the function worth it?" and let the customer determine value.[35]

Larry Miles stressed putting a dollar sign on each main idea. Know how much your ideas are worth. Never try to evaluate them until you have some idea of the possible dividends in return for your invested time.

---

35 Written by Larry Miles, circa 1950, Extracted from his *Value Analysis Instructors Guide*, Complements of the General Electric Company.

Estimate the dollar value

After having written all of your ideas down on paper the next step is to estimate the dollar value of each idea in order that we might spend time in proportion to their value. This will permit the Company, and correctly so, to spend the most time on the idea worth the most money and not necessarily on the idea which is the easiest to develop.

Work on the impossible

Larry Miles felt you should have enough courage to work on the impossible. It has been said that nothing is impossible. Then, it was said later that nothing is impossible – some of the things are just a little more difficult. He believed that nothing is impossible. It is purely a question of just how much is it worth to do it.

Obviously it won't work

Work on those ideas that have an obvious reason why they won't work. Larry Miles espoused the belief that there are very few original ideas. Hence, an idea that you have, may have been brought forth hundreds or thousands of times before by those who saw an obvious reason why it wouldn't work.

If the reason is too obvious no one will do anything about it. Many times a small amount of effort expended on this type of idea will immediately overcome the obvious objection. Always keep your objective clearly in mind. Namely, how can you make it work? What is the objection? Define it clearly, and then overcome it.

It won't work

Many times you have heard people make the statement, "It won't work." Usually the person who knows the least about the subject at hand also speaks with the greatest authority. When you hear such a statement it might be true. It probably won't work *the way the individual is thinking of doing it.*

Analyze and evaluate

So, after you have had a creative session, assign a dollar value to each idea, and then try to develop all ideas while placing more emphasis on those ideas with the most profit potential. Do not eliminate ideas but try to develop them all. Eliminate ideas only by developing much superior ideas. Use a positive approach even after a creative session when you are judging ideas. Without this all is lost.

✳✳✳

Chapter 3 emphasized the opportunities to improve value by studying and reducing overhead costs without much impact on the product itself. However, according to a paper by Jim Wixson,[36] material cost is where the main dollars are. He says, "We have to focus on where the cost is. Because design features drive material costs, a comprehensive cost reduction effort must attack the material cost embedded in the product design. Value analysis is a powerful and effective tool for attacking material cost embedded in a product's design as well as helping to reduce variable overhead costs."

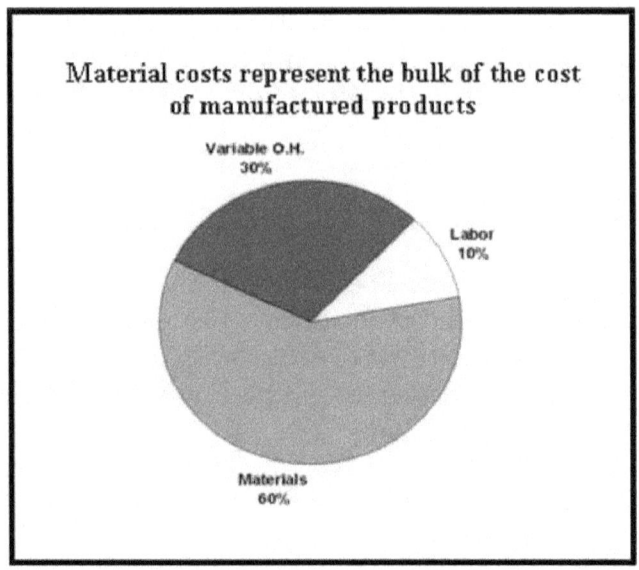

Additionally, VA is proactive in nature because it can be employed in the design phase of processes and products that will aid in avoiding serious problems later in production."

VA uses function analysis and FAST diagramming to describe the functional relationship of the product, process, or service and identify functions where the team should focus on improving value.

---

36 SAVE conference paper, 2005, *Value Analysis/Value Engineering – The Forgotten Lean Technique*, James R. Wixson, CVS®-Life, CMfgE, SAVE International Knowledge Bank, web site – http://www.value-eng.org/knowledge_bank/

"Creating by function is the high-octane fuel generating VA performance and success."

VA relies on a rigorous interdisciplinary approach to problem solving as illustrated below. VA uses a systems approach to problem identification and solution. VA is function oriented and promotes a "clean-sheet" approach that supports innovative solutions. Creativity is a key component to the VA problem solving activities that promotes "breakthrough thinking."

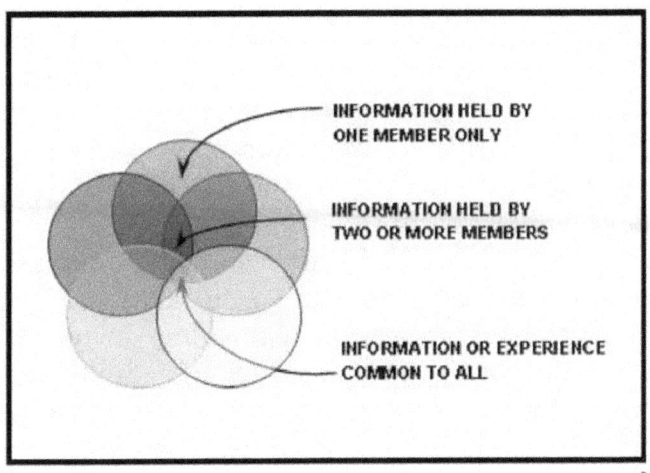

VA also uses a structured "job plan" that promotes consistency in application and helps assure results. Increased competitive advantage comes from the identification of innovative ways to accomplish key functions at a lower cost with improved quality and reliability. The function analysis systems technique (FAST) promotes a synergistic approach to problem solving that develops solutions far beyond that which only an individual could produce. These attributes combine to produce some superior advantages to problem solving when VA is employed.

✱✱✱

Value engineering is being used at the leading Consumer Healthcare global company – GlaxoSmithkline (GSK) Consumer Healthcare[37] as a tool to enhance the value of its products to its final customers/patients. GSK – a global manufacturer of name brand healthcare products such as Sensodyne toothpaste, Nicotine replacement smoking control products, and Tums antacid tablets, implemented its value program in 2011. Since that time, very significant value enhancements have been identified, primarily by looking at its existing product portfolio.

The most common tools used have been competitive tear-down analysis, function analysis and the mapping of consumer insights into product attributes and value. During tear down analysis, GSK compares the features and specs of its products versus similar internal products as well as against competition. This exercise has identified examples of over-engineering and waste as well as performance gaps in its products which when filled enhance value.

As an example, in GSK's nutritional drink business, a value workshop identified an opportunity to reduce bottle weight without impacting functionality. Consumer insight validation and factory testing confirmed consumer acceptability and manufacturability of the reduced weight bottles. As a result, GSK not only saved significant expense in unnecessary plastic costs, but also avoided the environmental impact of the energy consumption to produce the plastic equivalent to heating 132,000 homes for one day or about 250 car trips driven around the world.

Now that GSK's program has been established for two years, in addition to identifying and implementing value opportunities for current products, GSK's Value Engineering team within its Research and Development function is embedding a Design to Value approach into its product development cycle. Potential tools to enhance value include First House of Quality, review of Consumer complaints on similar internal products and competitive products, FAST diagram, and cost worth analysis of prototypes. These tools and other measures are meant to occur at set

---

37 Submitted by Samuel Maya, Director Value Engineering and Global Technical Support, GSK

milestones in the development process. By incorporating this approach, GSK is delivering the functionality the consumer truly wants in the most cost effective way possible.

✻✻✻

This Chapter began with the words of the originator of value analysis more than 70+ years ago. Since his day we have seen many ideas come into being, from TV to the smart phone. Whether they were original or just hitch-hiked on one another – who cares! Ideas create change and allow you to make more money!

You can make more money with value analysis because it allows you to invent on purpose, in a shorter time-frame than would otherwise be necessary. It does this by:

- Focusing on alternative ways to perform functions.
- Using a job plan to systematically go from development to implementation.
- Utilizing the best talent of your people.

The secret message in this –

You can identify the high cost functions in your products and find alternative ways to provide them using value analysis.

CHAPTER 10

Creating new products

Innovation can be accidental or deliberate. Value analysis speeds up the deliberate process and creates intentional innovation!

John Sloggy writes:[38] "The defining characteristic of our free market economy is Adam Smith's invisible hand continually pushing organizations towards higher levels of performance. You could call it the Wal-Mart effect. Prices must be lower, quality must be better, and production must be quicker. These characteristics have now become the price of entry into the competitive arena, but alone are insufficient to outperform our competitive rivals."

"What is required to achieve real profitability in today's marketplace is sustainable new product innovation. Innovation that

---

38 *The Value Methodology: A critical short term innovation strategy that drives long term performance*, John E. Sloggy, CVS®, SAVE International Knowledge Bank, web site – http://www.value-eng.org/knowledge_bank/

breaks the current competitive paradigm and establishes a new paradigm and the corresponding changes in profitability and market share. That kind of innovation requires the generation of creative thought that jumps the fences of existing paradigms."

He goes on to say that industry has a lot of tools to use that purport to solve every issue faced in the global competitive slug-fest. Multiple programs exist to support the manufacture of product with the goal of becoming and remaining a world class global competitor. Each tool has its proper application and often during its "day in the sun" the proponents claim that their program is the answer to all problems. How should you deal with the multitude of claims that are made in support of each program? When to use what tool is a question that many struggle with.

✳✳✳

LEAN manufacturing is a tool to eliminate or reduce waste. The theory behind LEAN is that if you remove waste you will improve flow and reduce variation and the associated costs. Variation affects the entire value stream. Reducing variation will provide more consistent yields and consequently higher profits.

Six Sigma is another tool in the box. The theory behind this tool is zero allowable variation. Again, if variation is reduced good things will happen as the process is brought under control. It is a process focused strategy and methodology for organization improvement.

- Old thinking: Come to work and perform our job to serve our customers.
- New thinking: Improve how we do our work to better serve our customers to stay ahead of the competition.

Six Sigma represents statistical thinking as applied to processes, variation and data. The focus is to improve process performance to enhance customer satisfaction and bottom line results; improving processes by reducing variation.

TOC, the Theory of Constraints is a tool to focus organizational efforts on system improvement, identifying constraints and eliminating bottlenecks. This will allow the system to flow at the desired capacity. It will eliminate the starts and stops and the corresponding excess inventory and inefficiency required to support production. Smoother flow and less just-in-case inventory equals higher profitability.

All of these tools are improvement methodologies. A particular improvement strategy may best fit the strengths and weaknesses of your organization's culture. All take the product/service configuration at face value and focus on improvement with the following assumptions:

- The design of product/service is essentially correct.
- The design of the product or service is the most economical.
- Customer needs are satisfied with the current design.
- The current design configuration fulfills the functional requirements of the market and customer.
- The management structure supports and nourishes change.

None of these tools, however, lead to enough innovation to sufficiently change the product to improve customer value or satisfy new customer needs. They merely "hold the fort," tweaking the given to make profit at the price points previously established. That is where the VA (value analysis) tool comes into play.

Dr. Jay Mandelbaum, a research staff member at the Institute for Defense Analysis (IDA) has studied the interaction of all of these tools. He explains in detail[39] the synergies between these tools and concludes that they work together comfortably to provide new, improved products and innovation.

✳✳✳

---

39 *Value Engineering Synergies with Lean Six Sigma,* co-authors Jay Mandelbaum – Anthony Hermes – Donald Parker – Heather Williams, CRC Press Taylor & Francis Group, 2012

VA differs from other methods in that it attempts to integrate the creative aspect into the problem solution. Not content to simply optimize the current solution, it searches for a new more effective design paradigm. A carefully orchestrated flow of information is presented that brings all participants to a common level of knowledge and encourages maximum creative output. It does this through the techniques of function analysis and function worth – coupled with creative techniques and supporting exercises. When done correctly, new solutions often emerge in a synthesis of new ideas that provide a higher quality synergistic solution than was possible without the VA process.

VA uses function analysis and FAST diagramming to describe the functional relationship of the product, process, or service and identify functions where the team should focus on improving value. Creating by function is the muscle generating VE performance and success. Function analysis is a forcing technique that allows the team to see the problem and corresponding solution from a different perspective that often results in creative solutions to the problem. It is proactive, seeking to develop new solutions to improve performance. Of course, when improperly implemented or rushed, VA techniques can be reduced to a structured version of cost reduction.

✳✳✳

A hierarchy exists that describes the impact a design has on an organization's resource expenditure. The design function to a large degree drives the company's innovation and consequently its long term performance. So, the best approach is to use the appropriate technique at the correct point in the product/project development cycle, as opposed to force fitting a specific process across all phases of the cycle. What follows is a hierarchy that represents the phases of the design development cycle: beginning with the identification of a need, identifying design objectives, design optimization and process optimization.

LEAN Manufacturing, Six Sigma and TOC address the labor and variable overhead segments of the cost structure, but have little or no impact on material cost, the largest segment of the pie. For the most part, design features of the product drive material and process costs, and the Lean/Six Sigma/TOC methodology offers little in the way of a tool kit for paring these costs. As design features drive material and process costs, a comprehensive improvement effort must attack the material cost embedded in the product design. Supply chain development programs will reduce price (and material cost) to a degree, but these efforts will always be limited by the underlying characteristics of the product design.

Value analysis is a powerful and effective tool for attacking material cost embedded in a product's design as well as helping to reduce overhead costs, resulting in real impact to the bottom line. It is proactive in nature in that it can be employed early in the design phase of products that will aid in avoiding serious problems later in the production cycle.

80% of a product's cost are dictated by the specific design. The greatest performance impact is achieved by altering the design of a product or project. While VA can certainly function as an improvement tool, its long term strength lies in discerning the needs of the customer and analyzing the functions proposed to meet those needs. It answers the 'how' question. It goes on to create a new combination of functions that create additional value for the customer by eliminating unnecessary functions or recombining and creating new functions.

✳✳✳

For the past 15 years Joe Otero[40] has run a highly successful Value Management (VM) program at his company, Pratt & Whitney. Since their reported 2002 success story of implementing over 14,000 ideas for the F135 jet engine for the Joint Strike Fighter and saving $500,000 on commercial engines without weight increase, they have been attempting to do VM earlier in design.

To quote Joe, "Since up front decisions impact value the greatest, it's imperative to address affordability in concept design."

---

40 Joseph F. Otero, Jr., CVS®, Value Methodology Integration Leader, Pratt & Whitney, United Technologies.

As shown in the chart below, design represents just 5% of the total product cost but represents 70% influence on total cost.

Jim Rains indicates that the meaning behind this chart is that most cost is created during product concept, yet companies do not know what cost they created until it is more expensive to correct it. Also, most companies do not use, give credit for, or believe in cost avoidance, thus there is no effort to save money during product development which is the best time to attack cost. I know that seems strange. They create the design and afterwards determine the cost. In target costing, the required cost is determined before the design. That way one insures profit.

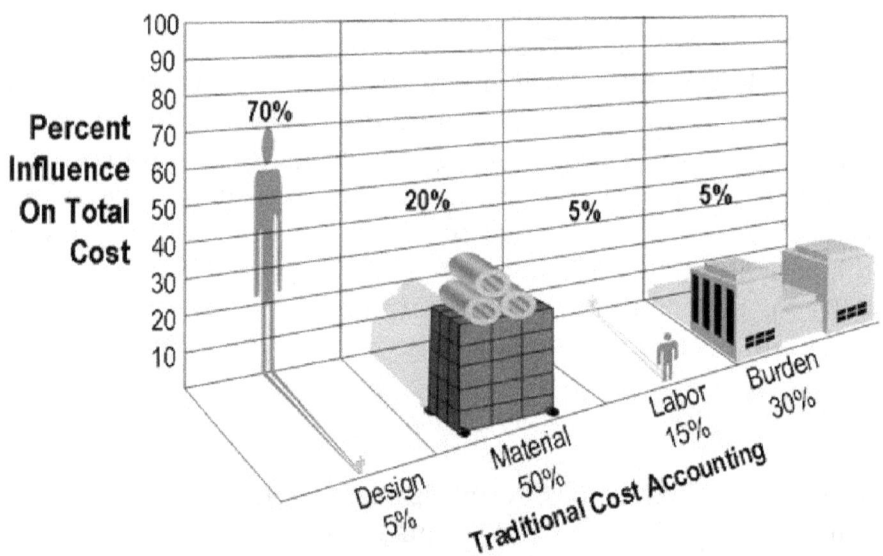

The strategy is to create performance/cost/weight relationships and link them to affordability initiatives for the client. The goal is to deliver essential functions in the most profitable manner.

When you pull VM into conceptual design you avoid problems instead of fixing them. Some favor using ranges of performance acceptability (versus hard points). This increases the potential to balance business needs with customer expectations.

✳✳✳

As shown below by John Sloggy, integrating the steps of the typical product development timeline with the above mentioned improvement processes results in the following diagram. This illustrates the most efficient point of application in the product development process. One can now see the strengths of each application and the importance of recognizing the correct application for the appropriate phase of product development. Organizational confusion can result from implementing multiple tools that attack the same overall goal from different avenues.

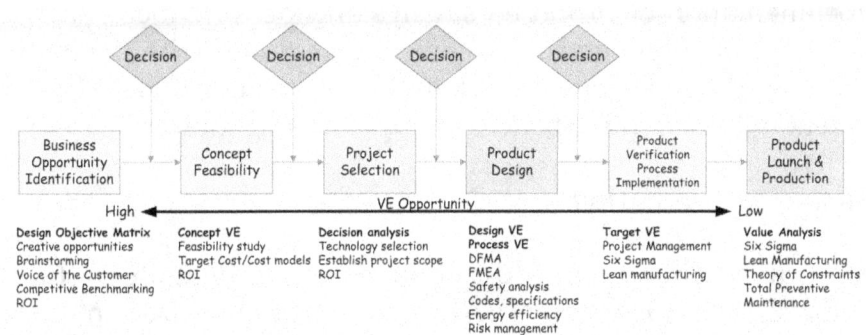

Product innovation is what separates high performing organizations from the rest of the pack. VA provides the vehicle to accelerate past the competition and reestablish dominance in business. It is the right tool for the times, and when utilized in conjunction with the Six-Sigma/Lean/TOC quality focus it provides a viable solution to today's intensive competitive challenges. From a public sector standpoint, the same benefits of a creative approach to problem solving provide unique solutions that are cost effective in these times of dwindling resources and conflicting priorities.

Organizations that pursue innovation as a competitive strategy need to inculcate it into their core organizational competencies. The VA process can be integrated into an organization's new product development (NPD) process at the concept stage to insure an early focus on innovation that permeates the organization.

Dr. Don Gerhardt wrote a paper[41] on the integration of VA with NPD at Ingersoll-Rand Company. He states that "an organization's ability to consistently develop high value products for its consumers is paramount for survival."

An intense, focused VA workshop of 5 days can jumpstart the creative process and leap the fences erected by existing design paradigms. A well run VA program is typically well received by participants and serves as a jolt to the organization's creative system. It can function as the catalyst for high performing teams.

Early stage VA workshops are focused on creative solutions to the identified external functions and as such may lack definitive documentation of proposed savings and performance enhancements. An enlightened management is required with the understanding that investing a week in the early stage of NPD has the potential to reap huge benefits for the organization.

Managing innovation

Innovation can be pursued as both a long term strategy (R&D) and a short term strategy (VA) to insure the organization's profitability and survival. While the traditional R&D function pursues innovation with a longer horizon, VA has the potential to fill the development pipeline with immediate innovation with both short and long term potential.

VA should be a central strategic component in the organization's effort to manage innovation. It has the potential to become the critical driver of innovation for an organization, and is the best investment an organization can make with its scarce human

41 *Ingersoll-Rand uses VE in New Product Development – A strategy for Business Survival in the 21st Century*, Don J. Gerhardt, Ph.D., PE, CVS®, SAVE International Knowledge Bank, web site – http://www.value-eng.org/knowledge_bank/

capital. What better use of that human capital than a one week VA workshop that could potentially identify a market changing innovation? At the very least the value of the design will be improved, sometimes dramatically, easily justifying the investment in VA. This requires the application of VA during the concept stage of design development to insure maximum flexibility in deciding the design direction.

Conclusion

Current popular approaches to improving an organization's performance (Six Sigma, LEAN, TOC) focus on optimizing existing designs and processes. While certainly a worthy and necessary endeavor, these techniques fail to address the existing design, which dictates up to 80% of cost and performance. That requires real innovation that can be addressed through the value methodology at various stages of the NPD process.

The development hierarchy demonstrates that VA operates on a different level than other optimization processes and as such should be classified as an innovation process. When coupled with the concept stage of NPD, VA has the potential to become an organization's short term innovation strategy, with real implications for a profitable long term performance.

A VA study that is rushed, late in the design process or improperly staffed simply cannot have a major impact on the direction, cost or functionality of a product. Rather than becoming a creative lever it is treated as a millstone for the design team. No one wants to add that kind of delay to a project. We all know the benefits of a well planned creative approach to the outcome of a project. This is exactly what VA can deliver. VA is about creating real value and making you more money.

The secret message in this -

You can invent new ways to achieve the functions customers want through your products by using value analysis.

CHAPTER 11

The Inside Job!

If you do it yourself you get all the credit and have no one else to blame!

Creating change is akin to changing culture in an organization. The only one that can do that best is the owner or top executive. There are three essential ingredients to create change. These are –

Executive involvement
Substantive investment
Systematic effort

If the boss doesn't want it to happen, it won't happen. If the boss doesn't show he really wants it to happen the effort to make it happen will be weak and fizzle. Change starts with leadership and is sustained by leadership. The executive must let the employees know that what is good for the company is good for their jobs and whatever improves profitability supports their jobs.

Substantive investment means willing to spend, to save and achieve that 10:1 return-on-investment (ROI) that VA is historically known for. You need to spend money on training, conducting studies, developing ideas, testing, and implementing change to get the reward at the end of the rainbow.

Systematic effort means having no sacred cows in your organization. Everything is an acceptable target for change. Systematic means prioritizing your savings opportunities, following up on value mismatches in the market, and using the VA orderly job plan to invent on purpose, in a short time frame, to improve profits.

$$***$$

To have a chance at being successful in implementing a VA culture, an organization must have a champion of the technique appointed by the executive. The champion must be allowed to directly interface with all other departments of the company – finance, engineering, manufacturing, purchasing, and marketing.

Larry Miles began his program in the Purchasing Department of the General Electric Company. From his manufacturing background and experience he states in his book[42] that "the essential work content of the operating value analysts is fourfold;

1. *Integration.* Making sure that everyone in the "environment" knows, in general, what it is, what it proposes to do, how it is to be done, how it affects them, how it can assist them to reach higher accomplishment in their work, and what other effect it will or will not have on them.
2. *Value appraisal and product or service evaluation.* Examining the existing product or service, using the system to remove costs and update the product or service.

---

42 *Techniques of Value Analysis and Engineering, 3rd edition,* Lawrence D. Miles, Lawrence D. Miles Value Foundation, 1989. pg 282

3. *Value consultation.* Assisting others who are in the process of creating a new product or service.
4. *Value analyses technique and system training.* Conducting a suitable number of appropriate courses for others so that the earnings competence of their companies will constantly increase or, if they are a service, the functions secured per dollar will constantly and permanently increase."

✱✱✱

Following are the steps taken outlined in a paper written by Jim Bolton,[43] who established a highly successful value program at the Whirlpool Corporation. Bolton writes, "How does one develop or expand an internal value methodology process in a manufacturing organization? Many manufacturing organizations that have tried to do this have failed, or, may get one going temporarily, but soon it loses momentum and dies a slow and torturous death in favor of the next newer process which promises to drive value for that organization."

He indicates that the key to the development of an internal manufacturing VA process is top management commitment. Without dedicated upper management commitment and an understanding of the principles of the value methodology, a successful long-term internal VA process can't be maintained in the manufacturing sector. Many manufacturing executives associate VA with cost reduction, and although cost reduction is often the result, it is by no means equivalent to VA.

In his opinion, an internal VA process for a manufacturing organization must be driven from the top down such that it is integrated within the total corporate strategy of that company. The manufacturing organizations which have integrated the VA process into their corporate strategy and product development process are the ones which will be able to not only initiate, but also sustain that process over the long haul. An internal VA

43 *How to establish and internal VA process in a manufacturing organization*, James D. Bolton, PE, CVS®, PVA, SAVE International Knowledge Bank, web site – http://www.value-eng.org/knowledge_bank/

process will drive total product cost leadership and deliver the ultimate value to that manufacturing organization's shareholders, trade partners, and final end users.

Besides increasing market share globally, an internal VA process in a manufacturing organization will train others how to think about value which enhances the number of loyal customers who will drive further growth, because, it's not just about cost.

Step 1 - Expose management

One of the keys to obtaining true management commitment and support for the VA process is to have the top executives in a manufacturing organization participate in a 40- hour SAVE International Module I workshop where a well balanced cross-functional team is secured. During this training, the VA process will not only be explained in detail along with the benefits of utilizing this approach, but the team members will have a chance to obtain hands-on experience using function analysis tools which are the heart and soul of this methodology.

This initial VA Workshop must be led by a certified value specialist (CVS®)[44] who has demonstrated successful results from previous studies delivering value to the manufacturing organizations and its customers.

Once the top management understands VA and its powerful function analysis approach utilizing a cross-functional team, they will be able to appreciate that if their products and processes are subjected to this methodology, major long-term benefits will be generated to enhance value to their organization.

Value is not measured at the time of the initial sale. Value is the performance of the required function measured over the intended lifespan of the product. If a manufacturer has the lowest initial price in the market for any given product, but the highest warranty and repair cost over the intended life of the product then the customer doesn't receive the best value.

---

44 SAVE International Certified Value Specialist. Listing found on their web site - http://www.value-eng.org/professionals.php

In addition to adding value for their customers, many patented products and processes are unveiled as a result of correctly applying the function analysis approach. Once these principles are understood by the top executives it is much easier to achieve the necessary commitment to use this technique for all of its products and processes globally and to establish an internal manufacturing VA process dedicated to improving the company's product cost leadership.

This sounds simple, but this will be the most difficult task in establishing and developing a successful internal VA process for a manufacturing organization. Without this fundamental knowledge of the total benefits that VA offers to a company, a long-term internal VA process will surely be difficult to establish or will eventually fail as that organization undergoes downsizing, which has happened in recent years with the current economic challenges.

Step 2 – Find your champion

Once the top management understands the total benefits of the VA process, they need to either hire a certified VA professional or develop an internal manager to head up their program. In selecting this manager, organization should seek to locate a VA professional who holds a CVS® certification and a Module I certification so that they are not only capable of leading internal VA studies, but will also have the ability to certify those that participate in these studies in the use and application of the various VA tools.

If the organization can't find such an individual or decides to look internally for a candidate to lead its internal VA process, there are certain qualifications which would be desirable for this individual. Someone with a good product and process background is highly desirable, and someone with an appreciation for industrial engineering or the costing of products and processes is also desirable.

This manager's first step, if not already trained in a 40-hour SAVE International Module I workshop, is to participate in such a workshop at a remote site, or to hire a VA professional to facilitate this workshop on-site with products and or processes that are manufactured by his own company.

The on-site training is superior to the off-site training, since the VA workshop will focus on a specific product or process, and it might as well be a product or process that the manager is familiar with rather than one for which he has little interest.

Step 3 – Select your first Project

If an on-site Module I[45] training workshop is selected, the organization needs to determine what product or process needs to be studied for this workshop. This may be a difficult decision, but the selection should be based on a variety of criteria. Some of those criteria include the profitability of the product or process in question, the complexity of the product or process, the importance of the product or process to the overall long-term growth of the company, and how much longer this particular product or process will be utilized before it is either replaced or cancelled.

First, it is important to select a product where the organization needs to improve its profitability, where the product is strategic to the long-term success of the company, and where the product is expected to be in production for at least two years or more. It would also be beneficial to study a product which is in the early concept phase, since the opportunity for improvement potential is the greatest. This is because the further down the development path for any given product or process, the more money is spent for concept drawings, prototypes, supplier or in-house tooling, engineering and development costs including validation testing, etc., and thus, any savings that are identified must now be offset with the additional cost to perform these functions again.

Step 4 - Select the first Study Team

The next step in developing an in-house VA process is to select a project study team. This will be determined by the product

---

45 Standards for a Module 1 workshop are set by SAVE International for its certification program.

or process selected, but no matter what product or process is selected, a cross-functional, multi-disciplined team is imperative. This means, that the study team should have ideally 6-8 team members from such areas as product (or process) design, manufacturing, process (or production) engineering, purchasing, sales (or marketing), program management (product or process team leader), and finance (or cost estimating).

This cross-functional team should all have a vested interest in the project being studied, where their input will have an impact on the outcome of the workshop. In addition, all participants must be 'team players', whereby they respect the views of other team members even if their views may strongly disagree. This is an important and possibly difficult task to accomplish, especially if you don't have any knowledge on how the potential participants may react with others chosen for the team. Nevertheless, this blending of personalities is of utmost importance for a truly successful VA workshop.

One key will be to invite people at the same level within the organization rather than members from different levels, where a senior level manager might intimidate a lower level member of the team. This is especially important during the creativity phase of the workshop and could really limit the team's success during this activity. In addition, it is often a good idea to invite someone from a totally different product or process area. Those who have a completely different type of experience will also help the team to potentially generate some fresh ideas. The experts on the team may not be able to 'see the forest from the trees' as they are too close to the project being studied.

As you develop the workshop study team, if you seek to follow these guidelines, the chances of a really successful event that will drive real value to your customers will be enhanced.

Step 5 – Plan to follow the value job plan

After identification of the project and the cross-function workshop study team is selected, the organization must adhere to the VA job plan if they are going to be successful in achieving the best project value.

Although this job plan may vary somewhat from company to company and project to project, all VA job plans must have the minimum of five different and distinct phases as follows: 1) Pre-Workshop, 2) Function Phase, 3) Creativity Phase, 4) Evaluation Phase, and 5) Development Phase.

Some VA professional's will combine the Information Phase with the Function Phase, and others will combine the Development (or Recommendation Phase as is often used) and the Implementation and Follow-up Phases, however, the author thinks it best to keep them separate because they have important differences.

When establishing an internal VA process for a manufacturing organization, it is best to keep the Implementation Phase and the Follow-Up Phase as separate phases since no real value is accomplished until the ideas from a VA workshop are put into production and monitored for a certain length of time to ensure success.

Step 6 – Conduct the Pre-Workshop Activities

Although some VA professionals may not refer to pre-workshop activities as a separate phase in the VA job plan, Whirlpool, for example, considers it the most important phase to guarantee success when utilizing the VA process. There are a variety of important pre-workshop activities, some of which have already been described which are absolutely critical to the success for any VA study. These include such things as:

Pre-Workshop Activities for a Manufacturing VA Study

Selection of Project to be studied
Selection of Project Team
Workshop Location, Date, and Time
Gathering of Data for the Information Phase
A pre-workshop team meeting should be held a minimum of two weeks prior to the actual VA Workshop. If it is

not convenient for all team members to attend this meeting in person, a conference call may be scheduled to ensure that all of this information is secured prior to the workshop.

There are advantages of selecting the actual manufacturing site of the studied product for the VA Workshop as access to the assembly or process line is easier, however, the disadvantage is that the manufacturing or process engineers engaged in the study may be pulled out of the workshop if a process crisis happens during this workshop. I personally seek to always have the VA Workshop facilitated at the actual site where the product or process is manufactured in order to permit the complete workshop team to engage in a line walk as part of the Information Phase of the workshop. In addition, it also ensures that the marketing and purchasing representatives have the opportunity to review the actual manufacturing process.

The next item of importance that is part of the pre-workshop activities is determining the time and date for the actual VA study. A complete VA study can't be properly facilitated in less than three days in the author's opinion, and those days should be in sequential order as the VA process is a building block process, and gaps in between each major phase really degrade the success of the workshop. Therefore, a date should be selected such that the complete workshop team can dedicate a 3-day block of time to focus on the actual product or process being studied. A time should be selected to accommodate all of the participants comfortably, that works for the manufacturing plant and does not interfere with it's work shift schedules.

Finally, all of the information mentioned in the Information Phase below must be gathered by the workshop team members and submitted to the VA Workshop facilitator, so that he may add this data to the individual team workbooks which each team member receives at the actual workshop. If all of this information is not secured prior to the workshop, it will be very difficult to be successful with the VA process. It can't be overemphasized - the need to complete the preparation of this information prior to the actual workshop. In the author's opinion, 50% of the success rate of the VA workshop depends upon the proper collection and distribution of this data.

Step 7 – Information phase

The workshop facilitator has the responsibility to gather from the VA Workshop team members a variety of information which is critical for all team members to be familiar with during the Information Phase. This information shown below should be assigned to the appropriate team members to submit to the workshop facilitator prior to the actual VA workshop such that team workbooks may be distributed during the workshop.

Information Required for a Manufacturing VA Study

Marketing data with voice of the customer input
Customer statement of work (requirements document)
A priced bill of material with material and process type identified all parts
Supplier footprint identifying manufacturing locations for purchased parts
Competitive analysis data based upon the project being studied
Any target costing objectives for the studied project
Drawings of all components (or sub-processes)
Descriptions for each station of the manufacturing production process Sample or prototype components (if available) for process workshops
Plant layout and flow chart of process
Design or process – Failure Mode and Effect Analysis
Finite element analysis or mold flow (or process flow) studies
Internal design, code, and legislative (or process) specifications
Summary of design (or process) quality or warranty problems
Test (validation) results for studied design or process

Step 8 – Conducting the workshop

The next job for the VA team leader of a manufacturing organization is to conduct the actual VA workshop itself. A good facilitator lays down some strict rules at the beginning of the workshop and then enforces them during the workshop without exception.

First, due to the fact that the VA process is a building block process with the following phases depending on the proper execution of the previous phases, you must expect complete participation from all team members for the total length of the workshop.

Second, don't allow cell phones or pagers or computers to be turned on during the workshop with the exception of one computer that may be required for accessing necessary data. There are sufficient breaks planned in the workshop agenda to make important calls and check e-mails. These types of distractions can adversely affect the effectiveness of the VA process and/or the facilitator.

Third, strongly encourage participation from all team members while in the workshop by requiring various team members to review with the whole team data they supplied for the VA workbooks and by asking specific questions of team members who seem to be just 'going along for the ride.'

If a VA workshop is going to be effective in the long term, then it needs the participation from all of the cross-functional team members, so that everyone feels they participated in the VA process and the results from that process. Each discipline represented on the workshop team offers a different experience that will help the team to better understand how true value may be achieved.

Finally, and most importantly, it is the internal manufacturing facilitator's responsibility to ensure that the VA job plan, with all of the phases, are followed implicitly without compromise. If any phases are skipped, the success of the VA job plan will be severely hampered if not totally destroyed.

Step 9 – The function phase

The most important phase for the VA facilitator to conduct properly is the function phase of the workshop. This can be done initially with the training of participants in the basic terms of the function analysis process including basic, secondary, supporting, unnecessary, design, all-the-time, higher, and lower order functions. It is then important to explain the function analysis process and the method of describing functions with an "active verb" and a "measurable noun".

This step of identifying and classifying functions is critical to the success of the workshop. Next, the use of various function analysis tools such as FAST diagrams or Cost/Function Worksheets need to be discussed, and those tools that the facilitator is most comfortable with should be employed in this stage of the workshop. I personally find that both of these tools are very helpful during the function analysis phase, and I always require every team to create their own FAST Diagram and Cost/ Function Worksheet even if other teams have generated these tools for similar products.

It is important that the internal manufacturing VA facilitator reinforces the two word function analysis techniques and stresses that specific component or process names not be used to describe a function. In the author's opinion, all VA study teams should attempt to complete a FAST diagram for the product or process that is being studied. The benefits of understanding the product or process from a function and logic point of view are so evident when using a FAST diagram that any study without such a diagram will struggle to achieve the maximum potential for the company involved.

If the cost/function worksheet is utilized, each component of the product or process being studied needs to have a cost assigned to all those functions identified that may have a relationship to that component. The cost/function worksheet technique helps to prioritize which functions have the highest cost impact on the product or process being evaluated. This information can then help identify those functions that have the highest cost, and thus, will be selected for further study in the next phase of the workshop, that of the creativity phase.

Step 10 –The creative phase

Although most facilitators can conduct a creativity activity, the creative phase using the VA job plan needs some explanation and VA training. A good VA facilitator will provide the workshop team with some basic training on brainstorming and other creative activities, but the most important part of the VA creativity phase is to conduct this phase by function rather than by component or process or some other criteria. When brainstorming in this phase of the workshop, ideas for each function must be identified based on the most expensive function as identified in the Cost/Function Worksheet down to the least expensive functions. A potential goal during this creativity phase is to develop a minimum of 50 ideas for each function identified on the Cost/ Function Worksheet or until all ideas related to that function have been brought forward. In this manner, if all functions on the Cost/Function Worksheet can't be brainstormed due to time constraints, at least those functions, which have the highest cost, and thus, represent the greatest impact to the final product or process are evaluated.

It is important for the facilitator to make sure that no criticism or evaluation of the ideas generated is done in this phase of the workshop. Once again, this requires the facilitator to be very strong in laying down the rules for participation such as not to hinder the creativity in this phase of the job plan. Many good ideas are never recorded or even spoken due to criticism being allowed in this phase of the job plan. In addition, it is important to emphasize that all members of the study team are equals in this workshop, and no idea is a dumb idea.

Exercising these principles may be difficult if not impossible to achieve especially if study team members are at different levels of management or have different levels of experience, however, it will be the facilitator's responsibility to make sure that all ideas are recorded for all to see and that all team members participate. Be sure not to limit this part of the job plan when ideas stop flowing freely. Continue to ask the 'how else', 'where else', and 'what if' questions for each function developed in the previous phase of the job plan. At least 25% of the overall allotted time for a workshop should be spent in the creativity by function phase. 'Piggyback,' 'hitchhike,' or 'expand' on ideas already recorded to generate slightly different ideas, and try not to quit until you have 50 ideas for each major function. If you use this method and follow these guidelines specifically, one will have a successful creativity job plan for the product or process under study.

Step 11 – The evaluation phase

There are many ways to conduct an evaluation phase in a VA process, however, the internal facilitator needs to develop a procedure that is comfortable and will meet the needs of that organization. One method that is commonly employed to evaluate ideas from the creativity phase is the cost-ranking matrix.

Cost Ranking Matrix

RUNNING CHANGE	SHORT TERM	LONG TERM
A	B	C
D	E	F

In this process, ideas may be ranked into an 'A' 'B' 'C' 'D' 'E' or 'F' category based on potential savings and speed of implementation. If the idea can be implemented fairly quickly "on the run" during production (within a 3-6 month window) with minimum investment, the idea is usually ranked as an 'A' idea. If an idea has high potential savings but will require tooling changes, validation, and customer approval, then it might be ranked a 'B' idea as it most likely will take longer than 3-6 months to implement. If an idea has major customer interface or technical challenges yet has high potential savings, then this idea might be ranked a 'C' idea.

Each manufactured product or process may dictate different criteria for the ranking of these ideas, however, the most important thing to remember, is to use the same criteria for all ideas. Those ideas with smaller savings potential should be ranked 'D', 'E', or 'F' ideas based upon timing. All ideas need to be ranked, and afterwards, included on a spreadsheet grouped by categories.

Step 12 – The development phase

This is the phase where a lot of VA projects get bogged down if not completely halted. I have found that the development of business cases where prioritized ideas are grouped together which could be implemented with the same resources in the same time frame and that will generate a specific payback for the manufacturing organization is the best method to obtain traction for ideas generated in the creativity phase. First, group the 'A' and 'D' ideas together, the 'B' and 'E' ideas together, and the 'C' and 'F' ideas together as it is best to combine high and low savings ideas together that can be executed within the same timing.

After all of the ideas from the creativity phase are grouped into categories with similar timing which could be validated with the same resources, then the development of business cases can be initiated. These business cases need to include the following:

a. A clear definition of the design or process changes recommended
b. The advantages, disadvantages, and associated costs for these changes
c. Capital and/or tooling required for change
d. Validation tests and associated costs to implement the idea
e. Customers affected by change and approvals required
f. A detailed listing of all the proposed design or process changes including:

1. Individual part numbers (P/N) or process numbers to be changed
2. Description of each P/N or process to be changed
3. The current and estimated cost of the design or process change
4. Any quantity differences per item from the current and proposed
5. The total annual volume that could be affected as a result of this change
6. Any supplier change for the current vs. proposed design or process
7. All savings such as labor or process reduction based upon proposed change
8. The team confidence level that the business case can be implemented
9. An implementation action plan with assigned responsibility and target dates

This allows one to calculate the overall savings per business case, the annual savings, the total investment required, and the payback for each business case.

Step 13 – Preparing the report

The next step in the development phase after all of the business cases are completed, is to have the VA leader organize and facilitate a management report-out meeting to gain management approval from the organization for resources which will be required to implement all of the business cases that are presented.

During this report-out meeting, the workshop team members should present the various business cases to the management team in enough detail to secure the required support to proceed with the actions in each business case. The complete workshop team should be in attendance for this management report-out meeting as well as the manager for each of the workshop team members and the plant management staff of the plant where the workshop was facilitated.

In addition, management team members who can make decisions for both financial and human resource allocation should be invited to participate in these management report-out meetings such that the project team leader can gain the support required to implement the business cases developed during the workshop. It is best to hold this meeting in the same room that the workshop was held immediately upon the workshop's conclusion. This retains the momentum of the workshop so that decisions can be made promptly enabling implementation plans to be executed without delay to achieve the timing predicted in the business cases.

Step 14 - Implementation Phase and Follow-up Phase

The global Design for Value Department at Whirlpool Corporation has responsibility for working with project teams to develop alternative concepts and technical solutions which can meet the target cost objectives established for any given product or process. Once these alternative concepts are developed via the business cases as mentioned above, they are then followed up by the project team leaders for implementation with the already established standard product development process used by Whirlpool globally.

Whirlpool's Design for Value (DFV) department is basically an engineering consulting group reporting to the engineering department whose main responsibility is to train and embed the VA process into the manufacturing organization such that the project teams have the ability to deliver the most cost competitive designs which will meet customer objectives at the best value. The project teams are then responsible for implementing the best ideas, concepts, and alternative solutions such that target costs are obtained for any given product or process. This VA process is proving to help the organization deliver cost effective products which meet customer expectations over the life cycle of the product.

✷✷✷

The above steps explain how a manufacturing organization can develop a successful internal VA process which can expand globally even during difficult economic conditions. A real key for the development and rapid growth of the internal VA process within Whirlpool Corporation has been the management report-out meetings after the completion of a VA Workshop.

Success breeds success, and once management commitment is obtained there will be a natural pull which will be created for this type of activity in all of the product categories globally for any manufacturing organization. The success of this VA process on several manufacturing projects within a few short months in various countries and on various products as facilitated by a VA specialist has shown that the VA process can work for any given situation.

This commitment and discipline to VA must be embedded into the culture of the manufacturing organization by incorporating it into the product development process for that company. Only then, will that manufacturing organization reap the benefits of implementing a successful internal VA process that will be self-sustaining in delivering the best value to its customers for the long-term.

The secret message in this -

You can improve the worth of your own employees by energizing them through value analysis to make you more money.

CHAPTER 12

Taking the risk!

You are taking risk every time you make money – the trick is to minimize and mitigate it rather than ignore it.

Being in business is in itself a risk you are taking. You can make or lose money for any number of reasons. I can only discuss here the reasons for risk that involve the product you are making or want to make, and are trying to sell. Those risks whether you know them or not are inherent in what you are currently producing.

Value analysis is in the business of creating change on purpose (alternative ways of performing a function). To many this is scary because change in itself represents risk. Often, for that reason alone many a good idea is turned down. The challenge of change is to manage it – to reasonably minimize and/or mitigate potential risks to gain the improved value from the change.

Up to this point, if you have performed a value study and have what you think is a good idea, all you have done is spend money.

You have risked the cost of the study. Until you implement something from the study neither you nor your customer will reap the benefits.

✳✳✳

This text will not be a treatise on Risk Management. There are many good texts on that subject. I will draw on one professional text[46] published by AACE International as a reference to the steps in Risk Management. These are:

1. Risk identification – Identify risks for the manufacturer and the user
2. Risk analysis – Determine qualitative and quantitative aspects and rate the factors
3. Risk treatment – Indicate how to deal with the risk
4. Risk control – Monitor your risk plan

In dealing with risk in value analysis you are only evaluating your current product with the prospect of modifying it, or, your current design or marketing plans with the intent of changing them for the better. Therefore, you need to establish a baseline for the risks being taken with your current product. This requires identifying the risk you now have for the product in terms of the risk involving items such as:

- Sources for raw materials
- Sources for purchased components
- Just in time delivery
- Labor skills availability
- Production capability
- Rework and failure potential
- Testing results

---

46 AACE® International Recommended Practice No. 63R-11, RISK TREATMENT, TCM Framework: 7.6 – Risk Management Rev. August 23, 2012

- Packaging, shipping and handling
- Customer satisfaction
- Warranty claims and recalls
- Etc. – add any additional risk areas as you see fit.

What is important is that you rate and score your current product, and your current plans that you are subjecting to change through value analysis. Then you will know how your new ideas stack up against the baseline you have already established.

✳✳✳

When you evaluate new ideas for risk you should do so only for ideas that serve the function and performance requirements of the user. Who cares what the risk is for ideas that don't meet the function needs and are not acceptable in the first place?

Authors Chang & Liou, in their paper on risk,[47] propose a simplified method, which combines the risk identification and analysis into the evaluation phase of the value job plan to examine the performance of alternatives. From their experience this method can help the VE team reach their consensus quickly on the best idea to implement, and it also documents enough information for the designer to complete the re-design drawings once it is accepted.

In VE studies, the Creative phase is a divergent phase that deliberately helps the team generate as many ideas as they can without first screening them. The screening is performed in the Evaluation or Judgment phase which is a convergent phase to assure only feasible ideas survive. In this phase of the study, the team judges and evaluates the ideas resulting from the creative session. The process typically involves the following steps:

---

47 SAVE conference paper, 2005, *IMPLEMENTING THE RISK ANALYSIS IN EVALUATION PHASE TO INCREASE THE PROJECT VALUE*, Yuh-Huei Chang, Ph.D., AVS & Ching-Song Liou, CVS® Life, SAVE International Knowledge Bank, web site – http://www.value-eng.org/knowledge_bank/

1. Eliminate nonsense or irrelvant ideas.
2. Group similar ideas by function within long term and short term implications.
3. Have one team member agree to "champion" each idea during further discussion and evaluation. If no team member so volunteers, the idea or concept is dropped.
4. List the advantages and disadvantages of each idea.
5. Rank the ideas within each category according to prioritized evaluation criteria using such techniques as indexing, numerical evaluation, weighted evaluation, and team consensus.
6. If competing combinations still exist, use matrix analysis to rank mutually exclusive ideas satisfying the same function. Make risk one of the evaluation factors to rank along with other factors such as: cost, performance, schedule, environmental impact, etc.
7. Select ideas for development for value improvement.
8. If none of the final combinations appear to satisfactorily meet the criteria, the value study team returns to the Creative phase.

✷✷✷

Once you have settled on an idea and have developed it, you then need to sell it. Present it to management for acceptance and implementation. Of course you will present all its benefits and features both technical and financial. You should also present the pros and cons of accepting the idea, and follow this up with why the con's of the idea should be ignored in favor of the pros.

Now is the time to discuss risk treatment! Management wants to know what risks they will be facing compared with staying with the status quo. Risk treatment involves classifying each risk as a threat or an opportunity and explaining one of the following four ways to deal with each risk:

Taking the risk!

Threat	Opportunity
Avoid	Exploit
Reduce	Share
Transfer	Enhance
Accept	Accept

The secret message in this -

The risk you take often affects the money you make.

Epilogue

Value analysis is not the only way to make more money. However, it is a deliberate accelerator of thought – at this time, on this project, at this moment!

It is a new way of thinking. Not everyone puts cost to function, but they should. Not everyone thinks about the worth of a function, but this gives the feeling, the insight into the realization of a value mismatch that has a chance of being improved.

It is a fantastic way of getting the customer to want your product, need your product, and value your product. The voice of the customer coupled with value analysis leads to new product development and more sales.

VA is effective in responding to customer complaints and reducing product repairs, replacement, and warranty cost. The value study of a product during design has collateral benefit in reducing errors and omissions in design documents and in spotting the need for changes before they become change orders.

The economic measure of value is life cycle cost. This is a win-win for both you and your customer. Products that perform as they are intended to perform, last as long as they are intended to last, have the mean-time-between-failure they are intended to have, and achieve the operating costs they are stated to have, are the products most valued by customers. With VA, customers pay for what they are getting and know what they are paying for.

The secret message in this -

VA is surely a way to make more money!

www.ingramcontent.com/pod-product-compliance
Lightning Source LLC
Chambersburg PA
CBHW051331170526
45166CB00002B/774